MW00423270

Get Recruited to Play Women's College Soccer

" A Step-By-Step Guide to Navigate the World of College Recruiting"

Lucia C. Bucklin

Published by: Ivy East Publishing
Greenwich, CT. 06830

© 2013 by Lucia C. Bucklin
Revised April 2020
All rights reserved world-wide.

All rights reserved. No part of this book may be reproduced, transmitted or given away in any form or by any means electronic or mechanical without prior written consent of the author, except by a reviewer who may quote brief passages in a review or article.

Cover photo - Shutterstock.com

ISBN: 978-9-9888769-1-0

Library of Congress: Copyright Office 1-877412381

Disclaimer:

Much of this informed published is based upon the personal experience of the author and represents their personal opinion and experience. Every effort has been made to ensure the book is as complete as accurate as possible and contains information on getting recruited only up to the date of publication.

The author and publisher shall not have any liability or responsibility to any person or entity, for any loss or damage which incurred as a consequence, directly or indirectly by this book, nor for any loss incurred as a result of specific decisions made by the reader.

The information provided is not guaranteed or warranted to produce particular results. The purpose of this book is to educate and should be used as a guide only. It is sold with the understanding that neither the author or publisher are providing legal advice or professional advice.

You agree to use this information at your own risk and hold the author harmless for any damages or loss from use or reliance on the information in this book. Every reasonable attempt has been made to ensure complete accuracy of the content, but the author and publisher assume no responsibility for errors or omissions, whether such occurs from negligence, accident, or any other cause.

DEDICATION:

To my wonderful husband, Robert, and my amazing daughters, Alexandra, Stephanie, Taylor and Alina. Thank you for all your help, support, love and patience while I wrote this book.

Thank you also to my daughters' soccer club coaches who provided invaluable advice as did the many college coaches we spoke to during my daughters' college visits and the recruiting process.

Get Recruited to Play Women's College Soccer

Introduction

Chapter 3 (Page 30)

Getting Started

...How big should my list of potential schools be?

...What additional things should I consider when picking
a school?

...What should I consider regarding the college athletic
soccer team?

...What is the best way to research the school's
soccer program?

...How many team players are in a certain position?

...How can my club coach help me with college recruitment?

...Am I being realistic about my ability?

Chapter 4 (Page 36)

What do College Coaches Look For in a Recruit?

...What catches a college coach's eye?

...What personal qualities do college coaches look for in
a student athlete?

...How important are my grades to a college coach?

...How good should my ACT or SAT scores be?

...How do coaches keep track of players they like?

...What turns off a college coach from recruiting a player?

...When should I be careful of when dealing with a
college coach?

...Why do some college coaches watch my warm-ups
as well as my games?

...Do I have to be with a top club to get recruited?

...What exactly is a Recruited Student Athlete?

...What do college coaches look for in a good Defender?

...What do college coaches look for in a good Goalkeeper?

...What do college coaches look for in a good Midfielder?

...What do college coaches look for in a good Forward?

...Is playing ODP important?

Chapter 5 (Page 45)

Your First Contact With a College Coach

...When should I start contacting college coaches?

...When should I contact a college coach about my upcoming visit?

...When can a college coach contact me?

...Recruiting Rules - Division I

...Recruiting Rules - Division II

...Recruiting Rules - Division III

...What should I say in my first e-mail to a college coach?

...Introductory E-mail *(example)*

...What do I write in my first contact letter to a college coach?

...Letter Example 1

...Letter Example 2

...How do I put together a good soccer resume?

...Soccer Resume Example

...What additional information does a college coach like to see?

...Is sending a DVD of my soccer highlights worthwhile?

...Is it best to talk to the head coach or an assistant coach?

...How will a college coach indicate early interest in me?

...How will a college coach pre-qualify me for their program?

...What does the information I receive from a college

coach mean?

...What questions should I ask a college coach on the phone?

...How much contact should I maintain with a college coach?

...What type of information should I keep sending a college coach?

...How important is my club coach's recommendation?

...Should I fill out a College Recruiting Questionnaire?

...Should I use a Recruiting service to help me with college coaches?

...When can a college coach officially contact me?

...What is considered a 'Contact'?

...What is the difference between a Contact period and an Evaluation period?

...What is a 'Dead period'?

...What should I do if a college coach contacts me and I'm not interested?

Chapter 6 (Page 68)

Visiting a College or University

...When should I start my college visits?

...When should I contact a coach about my upcoming visit?

...What is an Unofficial Visit?

...How many Unofficial Visits can I take?

...When is the best time to take Unofficial Visits?

...What happens on an Unofficial Visit?

...What is an Official Visit?

...When are Official Visits taken?

...How many Official Visits can I take?

...What happens on an Official Visit?

...When visiting a school, can I practice with the team?

Chapter 10 (Page 84)

Important Things to Consider When Picking a School

...Why is College roster size important?

...What is the turnover rate of players in the school?

...What is the coach's reputation with their team players?

...How long has the coach been there?

...How many players does the coach recruit each year?

...Why should I research the college team?

...What does it take to play at an Ivy League School?

...Will I require extra time to complete my degree?

Chapter 11 (Page 89)

Verbal Commitments

...What is a Verbal Commitment?

...When can I make a Verbal Commitment?

...How binding is a Verbal Commitment?

...What happens if I change my mind after verbally committing?

...Can a College coach change his mind after giving me a Verbal Commitment?

...How much time will a College coach give to me to verbally commit, if they are interested?

...What happens to my verbal commitment if I am injured before going to college?

...Is there a website that lists up-to-date college
commitments?

Chapter 12 (Page 93)

Athletic Scholarships

...Who normally gets an athletic scholarship?

...How do athletic scholarships work?

...When are athletic scholarships offered?

...What do athletic scholarships cover?

...Do college coaches usually give full athletic scholarships?

...What should I expect in terms of an athletic scholarship?

...Do athletic scholarships change year-to-year?

...Are multi-year athletic scholarships permitted?

...Can I lose my athletic scholarship?

...How is an athletic scholarship renewed?

...What happens to your athletic scholarship if you are
injured in college?

...If I'm unhappy at the school and want to transfer, can
I go to another school that's willing to offer me money?

...Do schools in the Ivy League offer athletic scholarships?

...Should my parents get involved in athletic scholarship talks?

...Should a player hold out for an athletic scholarship
to a school?

...If I'm offered an athletic scholarship, when should I
respond back?

Chapter 13 (page 106)

Your High School Transcript and ACTs/SATs

...When should I start to take standardized tests?

...What classes do I need to take to play college soccer?

...What High School classes are required with the NCAA?

...What are the advantages of taking the SAT's?

...What are the advantages of taking the ACT's?

...What is the biggest difference between the SAT and ACT?

...What do you need to know when taking the SAT or ACT?

...What are the average scores for SAT's and ACT's?

...Should I take Honors and/or Advanced Placement Classes?

...How important are my grades for admission if I'm
   playing college soccer?

...What do I need to play at an Ivy League School?

Chapter 14 (Page 112)

A Parent's Role

...Should my parents contact college coaches on my behalf?

...Can my parent's behavior hurt my college recruiting
   chances?

...What do my parents need to know?

Chapter 15 (Page 114)

Admissions Support

...How much support should I expect from a College Coach
   regarding Admissions?

...What is an Ivy Likely Letter?

...How do I register at the NCAA Eligibility Center?

...What happens after I register with the NCAA
   Eligibility Center?

...What happens if I need to talk to someone at NCAA?

...Do NCAA requirements apply if I want to play
   Division III soccer?

Chapter 18 (Page 125)

Different Types of Schools and Programs

...What does it take to play Division I Soccer?

...How many athletic scholarships are offered in Division I
   Women's Soccer?

...Which colleges offer Division I soccer?

...What are the Division I Soccer Conferences for Women?

...What does it take to play Division II Soccer?

...How many athletic scholarships are offered in Division II
   Women's Soccer?

...Which colleges offer Division II soccer and what are
   their Conferences?

...What does it take to play Division III soccer and do
   they offer athletic scholarships?

...Which schools are Division III and what are their
   Conferences?

...What is NAIA?

...What colleges offer NAIA Women's Soccer?

...What are the NAIA Conferences?

...Does NAIA Women's Soccer offer athletic scholarships?

...What is NJCAA?

...What colleges offer NJCAA Women's Soccer?

...NJCAA Colleges by Region

...How many athletic scholarships are offered in NJCAA
   Women's Soccer?

...What is NCCAA?

...What is NESCAC?

...What is required to play soccer if I am an
   International Student?

Chapter 19 (Page 133)

High School versus Club Soccer

...Do college coaches recruit from watching High
   School games?

...Do college coaches have a preference re: club vs.
   high school soccer?

...Can my club or high school coach help me with
   college recruitment?

Chapter 20 (Page 136)

Summer College Camps and Winter ID Camps

...Are college camps worth the investment?

...Are college soccer ID clinics worthwhile attending?

...Do college coaches really recruit players from camps?

...How can I figure out if a college camp is worthwhile
   attending?

Chapter 21 (Page139)

College Recruiting Showcase Tournaments

...How important are college recruiting showcases?

...What are some of the top recruiting showcases?

...When should I contact a college coach before a showcase?

...What should I send a college coach regarding my
   attendance at a showcase?

...What should I expect at a college recruiting showcase?

...What will a college coach be looking for when they
   watch you at a showcase?

...Should my club team have recruiting brochures to give
   to college coaches at a showcase?

...Should I send a thank-you note to college coaches
   who come to see me play?

...Is it a good idea to guest at College Recruiting Showcases?

Chapter 22 (Page 146)

Life as a College Soccer Player

...What are the perks of being a college athlete?

...When does college preseason usually begin?

...Do freshmen see a lot of playing time?

...Can I walk-on to a college soccer team?

...What should I expect with the speed of play in college?

...What will a typical year be like as a college athlete?

...What is a Student- Athletic Code of Conduct?

...What are the fitness standards in college?

...What should I expect in college play?

...How many players usually dress and travel with the team?

...What does it mean to be red-shirted?

...If I don't like my college, can I transfer to another school to play?

...If I signed a National Letter of Intent and then get a complete release, can I sign another NLI in the same year?

...What happens if I don't like my college coach?

...Can an athletic scholarship be withdrawn or reduced?

...How will a college coach decide an athletic scholarship the following year?

...What happens if my college coach leaves?

...How does a college coach decide who to play?

...What academic support is available to student athletes?

Chapter 23 (Page 157)

RPI Rankings and APR's

...What is an RPI Ranking?

...What is an APR? (Academic Progress Rate)

Chapter 24 (Page 159)

The NCAA Tournament

...What is the NCAA tournament and how are participating teams decided?

Chapter 25 (Page 161)

...Division I Colleges *(Women's Soccer)*

Chapter 26 (Page 163)

...Great Websites for College Recruiting Information

Author Biography (Page 167)

Introduction

Mary and her parents thought the time to get recruited to play Division I college soccer started in High School Junior or Senior year. It soon became apparent that Mary had started the process too late, and many college coaches had already committed most of their college roster spots to other high school student athletes.

Susan and her parents were more pro-active in the recruiting process. Starting Susan's Freshman year, she made a list of schools she was interested in academically and started to visit these schools. During her Sophomore year, she began contacting college coaches to come watch her play at showcase tournaments. Midway through her Junior year, Susan has numerous schools interested in her and was offered an athletic scholarship to play at one of her top college choices.

According to the NCAA, only 2% of athletes are actively recruited, leaving 98% to look for opportunities to play college soccer. Many athletes looking for information on the recruitment process in college soccer aren't sure where to turn to for advice. There are so many questions to ask, yet not one specific place to get all the answers. This is where *"Get Recruited to Play Women's College Soccer"* comes in.

If you're an athlete and want to play soccer at the college level, then you can't wait for coaches to come knocking at your door. Don't wait to be 'discovered.' The most successful players are the ones who take the initiative and start marketing themselves to college coaches as early as Freshman year in high school.

Many college coaches want to hear from good athletes who are genuinely interested in their program. They already know about the 'elite athletes', but they aren't enough of them to fill their roster, so they need additional student athletes. You must let these coaches know who you are and what you can offer.

The main thing to remember is that getting recruited is a multi-year journey that begins with preparation and a plan.

Chapter 1
Overview

The Sport of Soccer

Soccer is one of the most popular sports and played by millions around the world. According to FIFA statistics, nearly 265 million males and females around the globe play the game. The FIFA World Cup is the world's most widely viewed sporting event. An estimated 715.1 million people watched the final match of the 2006 FIFA World Cup in Germany, and the 2010 South Africa event was broadcast to 204 countries on 245 different channels. In comparison, in the United States, Super Bowl XLV (2011) averaged 111 million viewers.

Almost 40 years ago, there were no college athletic scholarships for women. Now, almost 200,000 women play college sports and many of those student athletes receive scholarships.

How many Women's College Soccer programs are there in the U.S?

Division I   333   Conferences - 32
Offer Athletic Scholarships

Division II   265   Conferences - 23
Offer Athletic Scholarships

Division III   440   Conferences - 49
Athletic Scholarships not offered

NAIA   188   Conferences - 28
Offer maximum 12 Athletic Scholarships per team

NJCAA   181   Regions - 57
Offer NJCAA DI Athletic Scholarships only

Total   1,407

* Information taken from NCAA, NAIA, NJCAA

What Athletic Scholarships are offered in Women's College Soccer?

NCAA Division I
...Offers 14 athletic scholarships for women's soccer

NCAA Division II
...Offers 9.9 athletic scholarships for women's soccer

NCAA Division III
...Does not offer athletic scholarships
   (Financial aid or academic scholarships only)

NAIA
...Offers up to 12 athletic scholarships for women's soccer

NJCAA Division I
...Offers up to 18 athletic scholarships for women's soccer

NJCAA Division III
...Does not offer athletic scholarships

Only a few elite athletes will receive full scholarships to play. It is more common for a College Coach to split scholarships amongst players (i.e. 1/2, 1/3, 1/4, etc.) for the team.

What percentage of kids go on to play college soccer?

Generally, there are only about 5,000 total roster spots available to freshmen at colleges *(Division I, Division II and Division III)*, and about 100,000 high school senior soccer players graduating each year. According to the NCAA, the 2% of athletes who are actively recruited are usually the elite or "blue-chip" athletes. It's a big deal to make a college team with or without an athletic scholarship.

Getting recruited to play college soccer generally involves two major steps. The first is to be offered a potential roster spot and the second is the athletics scholarship *(or academic funding)* discussion. The first step takes place usually before the second step.

What does it take to play college soccer?

You must have the talent to play at the college level. Second, you must have good work habits, maturity and self-discipline. Coaches look at academic performance in high school as much as they look at a player's skills on the field. If a player applies herself in the classroom, the academic success should follow in college. If you have the talent to play college soccer, you need to take the initiative to market yourself to college coaches.

The competition level in college soccer is high, at all levels. Division I is the most competitive, but even at Division III, NAIA or Junior College, the game is faster and more athletic than high school. College coaches are looking for the player who shows determination, dedication and passion. They want a team player who's willing to go the extra mile, has mental toughness, can perform under pressure and has respect for her teammates and coaching staff.

Tactical awareness is a huge plus. Coaches want to see a player who can read what is happening on the field and make the correct decisions to help her team. Physical speed is key. A college coach wants to see a player who displays speed, agility, quickness and strength by getting to the ball faster than her opponent. Some athletes are naturals at speed, but with others, it can be developed with consistent training.

Psychologically, can you handle pressure? Do you have the will to win? Are you not afraid of physical risk? College soccer is extremely physical. Are you willing to take on other bigger players going for the ball?

Being a college athlete requires a huge time commitment. Besides the 20-30 hours in class each week, you need to account for an additional 10-20 hours of team training (including fitness). On top of that, you need to add for travel time to matches and an additional 20-30 hours of study time.

Can playing soccer help me get into a better school?

Yes, to a certain degree, soccer can help you get admitted into a good school. Additional support from a coach can help a player in admissions; however, players must have the test scores and grades that are at least 'on the bubble' to get it. A coach only has so many 'pushes' with admissions, and the less they have to use with admissions, the better.

Coaches won't recruit a player with mediocre grades when it could affect the coach's graduation record or their own job stability.

That said, if a player has average grades, a coach can provide some support to an athlete to help in the admissions process. Admissions want to see that your grades are consistent and that you've been working hard in high school. A student with solid B's on her report card is perceived more favorably than someone whose grades range from A-C, as that tells the coach that the student is someone who has ability but may not have the discipline or motivation.

A student with solid B's, on the other hand, might be someone who steadily plugs away at her grades and makes certain the work gets done. The better the grades, the less amount of support the college coach has to use with admissions.

What is the difference between Division I, Division II and Division III play?

Division I is what most athletes are familiar with. Speed is the main thing that distinguish a Division I player from Division II, Division III and NAIA. The Division I player is required to do things much faster, as there is more pressure from other skilled players. Division I and Division II offer scholarships, while Division III doesn't. However, Division III offers financial aid in the form of grants, loans, awards, etc. Division II, NAIA and NJCCA *(Division I)* also offer athletic scholarships.

Division I requires a larger time commitment for the player *(with some exceptions like Ivy League Schools, which have time restrictions in place and a shorter pre-season).*

Athletes can easily spend 2-3 hours per day training and/or doing various other activities associated with the team *(fitness, playing in games, travelling to games, etc).* There is no off season in Division I. You are expected to train year round. The commitment in Division III is much less, as play in off-season is much more severely restricted.

Division I is very competitive, but there is quality of play in Division II and Division III as well. There are some top Division II and Division III teams, that could beat some lower level Division I teams. Travel times are usually much less in Division III, as games are usually closer geographically.

Chapter 2

The Recruiting Timeline

When should I start narrowing my choices and contacting colleges?

The recruiting process has begun so early, that many players are committing by the end of their Sophomore year, or early part of their Junior year. Many parents and players believe they have plenty of time, but often come to the conclusion that they should have started sooner.

If you have a number of schools you are considering, it's best to start the college visits as soon as possible, preferably as a Freshman. Visiting schools will give you a better idea of what you want, such as large vs. smaller schools, urban vs. rural/suburban, etc.

Develop a list of colleges in which you are interested. Don't worry if your list is unreasonably long *(20 - 25 schools)*. You want to make certain that you are not writing off any possibilities early in the game. Keep in mind that you should be happy with the school you ultimately choose.

A key question a soccer player should ask herself is *"Would I enjoy this school experience even if I did not play soccer here?"*

Freshman Year: You should start thinking about colleges. In 9th grade, you are considered a "Prospective Student Athlete" and can be identified and evaluated by college coaches.

Make a list of your top schools and do your research on them academically and athletically. Gather information on the head coach's name, e-mail address, phone number and mailing address as well as the school's soccer program. Draft a letter of introduction along with your resume to send to the coaches.

You may not get responses in your Freshman year, but you will start to get on a coach's radar, and more than likely, what you send is being reviewed. If you can, take the time to meet the coach, watch the team and learn more about the soccer program. As a soccer player, start to make a name for yourself on the playing field.

Sophomore Year: Start to visit the schools to get a feel for the campus. Contact the coaches and invite them to see you play. Review NCAA eligibility requirements and register with the NCAA Eligibility Center at the end of the school year *(see Chapter 17)*. As a soccer player, this is the year when coaches will begin to take serious notice of you.

Junior Year: By now, most coaches should have seen you play and will indicate their interest in you. If you're recruited by fall of Junior year, you're on their list of impact players. In January, they are looking to fill roster spots still open, but you may not be on their 'top list' of recruits.

Senior Year: The fall is the last chance to get recruited by a college. It will most likely be a Division III school, or in rare occasions, a Division I or Division II, whose potential recruit may have changed her mind. At this point, most NCAA

Division I money will have been committed.

What is the most important factor in choosing a college?

The number one priority should be a quality college education. Look for a school that meets your academic, athletic and social needs. If you were injured and couldn't play, would you still be happy attending that school?

Pick a school because you love it. Obtaining a good education should be the main factor in your selection. Your primary reason for going to college is to get a degree. Find a campus you love and where you can see yourself attending for the next four years. Does the school have your major area of concentration? Remember, you're a student first, and an athlete second.

Although a coach is important, they should not be the main factor in your choice of schools. You want someone who will motivate and challenge the team and be a great mentor. Get to know the coach's personality, communication style and philosophy. Do you prefer a coach who is very disciplined or more nurturing? What competitive level you want to play at? *(Division I, Division II, Division III, NAIA or NJCAA)*

When do schools start to recruit players?

On the girls' sides, recruiting is much earlier than the boy's side. It is also dependent on what Division (and to some degree, Conference) you plan on playing in.

Most of the bigger Division I schools typically recruit much earlier and it is not unusual for the top schools with excellent soccer programs to get verbal commitments during the beginning of a player's Junior year, or in some cases, their Sophomore year. However, these usually are the 'soccer studs' that play on a National or Regional team. They most likely will be the ones that are offered the highest in terms of athletic scholarship dollars.

Other Division I schools will usually finish off recruiting high school Juniors with the last push coming shortly after the Memorial Day Showcases. At that point, most of the money will be committed for that particular incoming group. It doesn't mean that the scholarship money has totally dried up, but the better-known soccer institutions have already made their decisions for that recruiting class.

Division III schools will usually decide on players in September/October of the player's senior year. Although coaches are looking for the best players, if the high school grades and test scores are not there, a coach will not be able to get you in. NAIA and NJCAA also have greater flexibility in recruiting at a later time.

Chapter 3
Getting Started

How big should my list of potential schools be?

Before you make your list, be honest with yourself and assess your strengths and weaknesses.

Draft a list of about 20-30 colleges that interest you. It may include schools in your area, or schools that have a particular major you are interested in. It might even include schools you know little about. The list may be long, but in the early stages, you don't want to eliminate any schools that seem interesting to you. Would you want to go to that college, even if you didn't make the soccer team?

You can further divide the list into three. The first list could consist of your dream schools, the second list the schools that you can realistically get into, and the third list, your fallback schools.

For each school in that list, create a sheet that has the coach's e-mail address, mailing address and phone number. That list should also include a list of the majors you are interested in at that school and their admission requirements.

What additional things should I consider when picking a school?

Besides your first priority of getting a great education, you can consider factors such as:

.....Do I want a large versus small campus?

.....Do I want an urban vs. rural environment?

.....What is the distance from home?

(Most students usually don't go further than 5 hours

from home)

.....What is the student-to-faculty radio?

.....What is the graduation rate for students?

.....How is transportation to the school?

(Is it easy to get to either flying or driving?)

.....What is public transportation at the school like?

.....What is the on-campus housing like?

.....What is the on-campus meal plan like?

(Some colleges offer unlimited dining, others can be 3 meals/day only. Some plans allow you to eat off campus)

.....What kind of climate/weather do I like?

.....What is the social environment like?

.....Do I have the required academics to get in?

What should I consider regarding the college athletic soccer team?

.....Do I want to play at a school with a winning record?

.....Would I be able to get a lot of playing time?

.....Would I be happy here, even if I was sitting on the bench and not playing much?

.....Do the coaches seem friendly, sincere and supportive with their athletes?

.....Would I still select the college if it had a different head coach?

.....Am I interested in playing Division I, Division II or Division III? Or do I want to play NAIA or NJCAA Soccer?

You could also consider smaller, lesser known schools if

you're a good player looking for a scholarship opportunity. These schools are always looking for talented athletes, as a large majority of top players prefer to go with a big-name school. Some smaller schools have great programs that could beat some lower level big school teams, and they have the money to pay for your education.

What is the best way to research the school's soccer program?

Often players will contact a coach and know nothing about the soccer team, the coach or the style of play. Do your research online about each individual school and look at their statistics for the past 3 years. Look at their wins, losses, which players have the most playing time *(are they the players with the strongest statistics or does the coach have some favorite players he/she constantly plays?)*

Is the roster size consistent or are players dropping out after a couple of years? Look at the number of Juniors and Seniors on the roster. If you don't see that many other than the starters, it may be that the coach doesn't care about the players and has a high turnover rate, or the players get burnt out.

Is the roster overly large? Some state schools stockpile 30+ players. It's rare for any player ranked towards the bottom to make a significant impact later. Does a coach stick with the same 11 players, even during blowout games, or do they give more players opportunities to play?

How many team players are in a certain position?

If you're a forward, and the team already has 6 forwards, chances are good that they may not need any more unless a majority of them are graduating soon. Questions to ask are:

.....What type of background do the players have? *(If a school is recruiting Regional and National level players, it will be harder to make the roster).*

.....How large is the roster? *(If too large, you may not see much playing time unless you're an immediate impact player).*

.....How long has the coach been there? *(If it's a new coach, then they should be there for the next few following years building the program).*

.....What is the coach's record? *(If he/she has been consistently losing over the past few years, they may not stay in their position much longer).*

It's recommended to go see that team play to see if your style of play matches theirs.   If a team plays a technical passing game with short touches, you probably won't fit in if you like to kick long balls as a player.

It helps to check out the existing roster of the college you are interested in. Looking at the current players' hometowns will give you insight into where the coach is focusing his/her recruiting efforts. Clicking on their profiles will give you further information on the competitive qualifications for the team.

According to BigSoccer.com *(Women's College Forum),* no college needs to carry more than 26 players and colleges usually travel with only 18 players.

How can my club coach help me with college recruitment?

The coaching community is actually a very tight knit network and you should inquire who your club coaches know well. Their recommendation is often a great "door opener."

Ask your club coach for an honest appraisal of what level of school they think you can play at. This will help you formulate your list of schools that you might want to attend, from a soccer point of view.

College coaches value the opinion of your club coach in the recruiting process. However, don't rely on them to do your recruiting for you. You alone should be responsible for your recruiting process. Club coaches can make calls on your behalf, but ultimately, getting recruited is your responsibility.

Am I being realistic about my ability?

One of the critical first steps is to identify the right academic school for your academic and athletic abilities. Target the schools where you have the best chance to compete for a spot on the team and receive a potential scholarship. Shooting too high or being unrealistic can considerably lessen your chances for a college career if you only look at schools above your talent level.

You may be able to play at top schools, without having an elite resume (*i.e. National team or Regional team experience*), but don't expect to be heavily recruited.

What do you want from your college experience? If you have the necessary tools to play at the Division I level (*tactical, technical, physical*), do you want to devote the time

34

and dedication? If you had to sit the bench for a few years at a Division I college program, would you be better off at a Division II, Division III, NAIA or NJCAA school where you can make an impact and enjoy the experiencing of playing college soccer?   Sometimes schools have been known to recruit a player just to keep them from other college coaches.

Chapter 4
What do College Coaches Look For in a Recruit?
What catches a college coach's eye?

When coaches walk up to a soccer field, the first things they will notice is how hard a player works and how competitive she is. They want to see a player compete with great energy and enthusiasm. They expect performance at a high level. They expect players to already know how to tackle hard, play defense and head the ball. They want to know that the player can win 50/50 balls and maintain possession of the ball.

Coaches like a player who isn't afraid of being physical on the field. They are looking for a player that shows potential for exceptional development through consistent coaching.

College coaches will be also be looking for a player who is strong in four key areas which are:

Physical: Speed, strength, power, agility, and cardio-vascular fitness. Can they easily pass all fitness tests? Being fit is a huge part of the game and a player's fitness tells the coach a lot about her attitude and commitment.

Technical: How sound is the player in all skill related areas, and can they play equally well with both feet?

Tactical: Coaches love players who understand the principles of play. Tactical skill is based on decision-making and intelligence.

Psychological: Is a player mentally tough? Are they relentless and persistent? Do they give up when it gets hard? If you break down after a tough play, most will write you off

36

their recruiting list. Is the player disciplined and focused? Are they a team player with a strong work ethic?

Some coaches will stay after a game to see how a player has handled her team losing. Does the player have a good attitude? Is she tough emotionally, or does she mentally break down by crying after a loss?

What personal qualities do college coaches look for in a student athlete?

College coaches look for clues to see what kind of person a potential athlete is. They place a lot of emphasis on a player's character.

.....How does that player treat their teammates and
their coach?

.....What kind of attitude do they have on the field towards
the referee?

.....How do they treat their parents?

.....Does that player give 100% effort?

.....Are they honest, reliable and dedicated?

.....Is the player coachable and is she mentally tough?

.....Are they a leader?

.....Do they engage in risky behavior with alcohol or drugs
(easy enough to check through Facebook!)

All these things say a lot about a potential player and can get you added to the list of recruits.....or dropped.

In today's electronic age, it's easy to monitor your behavior on Facebook or Twitter. Coaches don't want to see a potential recruit drinking or holding a little red cup in their

37

hand. Recruits who make poor decisions stand out from those who don't. Don't let bad personal choices hurt your scholarship possibilities.

As an athlete, you represent the school and are held to a higher standard. You can't control the people around you, but you can control how hard you work and the choices you make. Ultimately there is only one thing you can control -- and that is yourself.

How important are my grades to a college coach?

Grades are a lot more important than you think! Academics do a play a large role in getting recruited, but the criteria will vary school to school, based on the school's academic strength. Soccer will get you to the door but if you don't have good academics, you won't get in.

Coaches expect good grades from you, and those grades can make the biggest difference in admissions and financial aid outcomes. For most schools, having poor grades can mean failure in getting recruited. You must be prepared to work as hard academically as you do athletically.

Coaches want reasonable assurance that the athletes they recruit will not develop academic problems down the road, that could result in ineligibility, or dropping out of college altogether. Having good high school grades shows you are prepared and willing to work hard.

Some schools, besides offering a partial athlete scholarship, may supplement an athlete's package with academic scholarships. Good grades mean greater college choices, and your tuition costs will be much lower each year.

Division III institutions do not offer athletic scholarships, so your grades as just as important as your athletic skills in the recruiting process.

Even if players are incredibly talented, their grades can prevent them from getting a college scholarship. Coaches want someone who can pass admissions standards. Even with a verbal commitment early on, recruiting offers can be withdrawn because of low grades.

How good should my ACT or SAT scores be?

If you want to play for a top program with high academic standards, you most likely will need a great SAT or ACT score, unless you are a top level National Team player, where a coach can pull in some favors with the admissions dept. But even then, you won't be able to get in if you have failing grades or test scores. Check the school's admission standards on their website and you should be close to at least their minimum acceptance standard, although higher would be preferable.

How do coaches keep track of players they like?

When a coach comes across a player who has talent, good academic credentials, and the potential to make a difference on their team, they will usually add that player to a list or recruiting board in their office that is updated constantly, until the recruiting class is finalized. The list is usually organized by position and below is usually the player's name that the coach is interested in.

What turns off a college coach from recruiting a player?

There are a few things that will turn off a coach from pursuing a player. These are:

.....Asking about athletic scholarships before the coach even knows about you. *(You need to demonstrate to the coach how you can contribute to the team before you start to ask about money!)*

.....Over-exaggerating your resume. *(They'll wonder what else you're not being truthful about!)*

.....A player who sends out mass e-mails or letters to the coach. *(If you can't be bothered personalizing your letters or e-mails to the coach, do you really want to go to that school and play there?)*

.....Parents who get involved in the recruiting process for the player. *(The coach is recruiting the player, not the parent)*

.....The Diva player. *(No coach wants a player who thinks she is better than everyone else and has an attitude. It's all about respecting the team, the coach and working together).*

.....Inappropriate Facebook postings. *(No alcohol, no compromising photos, no reference to drugs no vulgar language, etc.)* Your character is in question, so keep everything clean. No coach wants a problem player!

.....Inappropriate Twitter postings. *(Character counts for a lot. Be respectful!)*

What should I be careful of when dealing with a college coach?

A good coach will be upfront with you about the possibility

of you playing for the team. After they see you play at a few tournaments, they will tell you where you stand on their recruiting list. They may even bring up a scholarship offer.

Beware of a coach who wants you to trust him and won't commit to a definite offer. It's sometimes hard to ask tough, specific questions of the coach, but you'll be happy you did as the coach will have to be more specific.

The last thing you need is to have a coach string you along, and then at the last minute decide they really don't need you and you have no options left with other schools.

Why do some college coaches watch my warm-ups as well as my games?

Some coaches will watch warm-ups to notice how hard a player works and how competitive they are. Do they approach the warm-ups with intensity and passion, or just go through the motions? They want to see a player who treats practice and warm-ups the same as in a game situation.

Do I have to be with a top club to get recruited?

College coaches recruit players not teams. They do care about how competitive your opponents are. It helps to play at the highest level and/or with the best club you can. However, it is how you play on the field that will determine the coach's interest. Many top clubs will have access to top showcase tournaments where many college coaches will be watching players to recruit.

What exactly is a Recruited Student Athlete?

NCAA rules state a player becomes a Recruited Student Athlete when they receive a telephone call from the coach, make an official visit, have an off-campus meeting with a coach or have received a National Letter of Intent.

What do college coaches look for in a good Defender?

Do you have the speed and quickness to keep up with some of the nation's top strikers? Can you win 50/50 challenges consistently? Can you play the ball out of the back, rather than just clearing it? Do you have the technical ability to accurately play long passes to your teammates? Do you have tactical awareness?

What do college coaches look for in a good Goalkeeper?

Are you a good leader and communicator with your back line? Do you have the technical ability to make 100% of saves in the middle, along with many of the bigger saves in the corner? Do you have command of your goal area? Do you have great distribution with your goal kicks and punts, along with back passes? Do you have speed and quickness? Do you work as hard in training as you do in games?

What do college coaches look for in a good Midfielder?

Are you in amazing shape *(superior fitness level)?* Do you have speed and quickness? Do you have superior passing skills? Can you play the ball from side to side, as well as back to front of the team? Do you have the tactical ability to read the game? Do you have a broad field of vision? Do you handle pressure well? Are you physically strong and agile? Can you attack and defend effectively?

What do college coaches look for in a good Forward?

One of the most important traits is physical speed. Can you break away from strong defenders? Do you have the confidence to take on players en route to goal? Do you have superior physical fitness? Are you comfortable with both feet while under pressure? Do you have the ability to hold and shield the ball with your head up, to allow your teammates time to move into position?

Is playing ODP Important?

ODP *(Olympic Development Program)* looks great on your soccer resume. Tryouts are open and are hold by birth year in every state. If you make the team *(generally about 25-40 kids, as some states have two teams at the younger age groups),* you are considered one of the best state players in your birth year.

Your state team will play other teams from other states in competition and at Regional camp *(held 1x/year in summer).* At Regional camp, coaches will pick the Regional pool and team. If selected, that means you are amongst the best players in your particular Region.

The Regional team competes against 3 other Regional teams in the U.S. If you make the Regional team, you're considered amongst the best 100 OPD players in the Nation. In addition, many of the National team *(and National pool players)* are selected from Regional play.

ODP shows that you've competed at a high level of soccer. Some players chose not to participate, as they feel the selection process is too political and subjective.

Chapter 5
Your First Contact With a College Coach

When should I start contacting college coaches?

Towards the end of your Freshmen year is a great time to start contacting college coaches. A student becomes a prospect starting in 9th grade.

Make certain that when you contact a college coach, you have their correct name, title, e-mail and address. College coaches can change jobs, and nothing turns off a college coach who sends a letter with incorrect spelling, a previous coach's name or even the name of the wrong school. Do your research!

When should I contact a college coach about my upcoming visit?

Give a coach adequate notice that you would like to visit *(usually 3-6 weeks)*. Start by calling the coach to talk about a potential visit. You should ask what dates would work best for the coach, and if they can take the time to meet with you.

When can a college coach contact me?

NCAA has strict recruiting rules that limit communication at tournaments. If a coach talks to you or your parents off campus *(i.e. a showcase tournament)*, and says anything more than hello, it is considered a contact.

Recruiting Rules - Division I

Coaches <u>are</u> allowed to contact your club coach at any time, to indicate they are interested in you.

Freshman and Sophomore Year

You are generally off limits to college coaches. Division I and Division II coaches can't call or e-mail you or have any contact with you <u>off</u> their campus. You can receive brochures for camps and questionnaires, but no personalized recruiting materials. You can make as many unofficial visits as you want. You may call the coach at your expense only; however, college coaches <u>cannot</u> return your call if you leave a message nor can they e-mail you. You can talk to a college coach only when visiting their campus. Official visits are not allowed

Junior Year

You can receive letters and -emails from college coaches interested in recruiting you as of Sept. 1st of your Junior year. Coaches can send you information about their athletic program and their school. You can call the coach at your expense; however, college coaches cannot call you or return your telephone calls. You may make as many unofficial visits as you want. Official visits are not allowed.

Starting July 1st after your high school junior year, coaches can make one call each week to you or your parents. Junior year is when most NCAA Division I money is allocated.

Senior year

Any in-person contact between you and your parents and a coach that goes beyond a basic "Hello" is allowed up to three times during your senior year. College coaches can't evaluate you more than 7 times during your Senior year.

Beginning opening day of your Senior year, you are allowed one official visit per college up to a maximum of 5 official visits to Division I and Division II schools. Each visit can't be longer than 48 hours. You can text a coach, but they cannot text you back until after you have signed your NLI *(National Letter of Intent)*.

Recruiting Rules - Division II

Division II rules are similar to Division I.

Recruiting Rules - Division III

You may receive recruiting material *(printed)* at any time as there are no rules when a coach can send you a letter stating they are interested in you. However, in most cases, Division III coaches will not send mail until the end of high school Junior year. You may call a coach at your expense, and there is no limit on the number of calls or when they can be made by the college coach. College coaches are allowed to contact your club coach at anytime, to indicate they are interested in you.

Regarding off campus contact, a college coach cannot have contact with you or your family until after your Junior year. NCAA voted *(Jan. 2012)* to allow text messaging *(for Division III)*, regulating it to the same standard as phone, email and fax correspondence in the recruiting process.

Official Visits: There is no limit as to how many colleges you can visit. However, you may make only one official visit per college starting with your first school day during high school Senior year. Some Division III schools do not offer official visits, and some may have limited recruiting budgets *(and therefore, may not be able to pay for a recruit's expenses to visit the school).* Other Division III schools can offer to pay for the cost of transportation, lodging, and meals.

NAIA Recruiting Rules

The NAIA *(National Association of Intercollegiate Athletes)* recruiting process for freshmen has less restrictions on contact between a player and a coach. NAIA schools offer athletic scholarships and are governed by different rules. Although NAIA has stringent academic requirements, eligibility is streamlined as there is no clearinghouse. All students who play to attend an NAIA school, must register with the NAIA Eligibility Center.

NAIA allows unlimited official visits, but only one per school *(visits shall not involve the loss of school time unless formal prior approval is obtained)* Communication can occur anytime, much like NCAA Division III rules.

NAIA schools may invite student-athletes to visit their campus and offer scholarships at any time.

NAIA schools permit a potential recruit to train with the team while on a campus visit *(which shall be limited to no more than two days for a specific student at a member institution).*

There is no signing date for NAIA, so players can sign a Letter of Intent at any time *(after which a student-athlete can train with the team whenever they are available).* In the event, if a player feels the school or team is not a right fit after playing there for the season, they are allowed to transfer to another NAIA institution and compete the following year without having to sit out a year.

Whatever Division you choose to play in, don't get discouraged if coaches don't initially respond during your Freshman and Sophomore year. In most cases, they cannot. If you are truly interested in a school, it is important to keep calling until you reach someone.

For all recruiting, don't expect college coaches to talk to you at events outside their school, as they will be following the no-contact rule for off -campus competitions until the end of your Junior Year. During Senior year, Off-Campus contact is permitted.

What should I say in my first e-mail to a college coach?

Don't send out an e-mail blast, but personalize your e-mail with the college coach's name, why you're interested in the school's soccer program and why you think you'd be a good fit for their team. You should let the coaches know your upcoming tournament schedule and invite them to see you play.

Make sure that your first contact is precise and tells the coach why you are interested in the school and the coach's program. Your tone should be formal *(no BFF language)* and all words should be spelled out, with proper grammar. Remember to spell-check before you send. You have only one chance to make a positive first impression. Show the coach you've done some research on the college by knowing the Conference they are in, their record, the team, etc.

Introductory E-mail (Example)

Dear Coach *(enter Coach's Last name):*

I have just begun the college search and *(enter University name)* is one of my preferred schools. I have attached my college soccer resume for you to review, as I am very interested in your program.

I currently play for *(enter Club name)* as a *(enter position).* I am a *(Freshman, Sophomore, Junior, etc)* at *(name of High School)* and a *(enter year of graduation)* recruit.

I hope you will have the opportunity to come and watch me play at one of my upcoming tournaments. I will keep you posted on our schedule once it becomes available. Currently, my club *(name of club)* is scheduled to play at *(list tournament schedule for year, such as Disney, PDA, etc).* Thank you for your consideration.

(Your name & email address)

What do I write in my first contact letter to a college coach?

The first contact letter will be very much like the first e-mail to the coach.

Do not address the letter as "Dear Coach", "Dear Sir/Madam", etc.; otherwise it comes across looking like a form letter. Address the coach by their surname, as in "Dear Coach Brown," and mention the College in the opening paragraph to show the letter is targeted towards the school.

Make certain that your information is current and correct. There is nothing worse than addressing a letter to a coach, only to find out that they left the year before. Don't write a letter like you're addressing it to your best friend. Keep it professional. Make certain it has no spelling or grammatical errors. *** Do your homework.

Tell the coach why you want to attend their school (*i.e. academics, coaching style, location, etc*) and what you'd bring to the team. Include your soccer resume and high school grades. You can close your letter by asking the coach about the possibility of seeing them on an unofficial visit and by inviting them to see you play.

Coaches are looking for letters that include the following:
.....Player's name
.....Name of high school
.....GPA and Graduation year
.....The Club you play for
.....Upcoming tournament schedule

Letter Example #1

Date

Coach *(Full name of Head Coach and Title)*
College/University Name
Mailing Address
City, State, Zip Code

Dear Coach *(Enter last name of Coach):*

As a *(enter your age)* year-old rising *(enter school year)* at *(enter high school)* who plays with *(enter club name),* I am very interested in attending *(enter name of University),* playing varsity soccer and potentially majoring in *(what you'd like to study).*

I've had the opportunity to research the academics at *(name of University)* as well as the soccer program. I feel that I can make a positive impact on your team.

I am *(enter soccer information here, such as the position you play, and your special qualities such as goals scored, save percentage if GK, awards you have won, highest level you have played at, etc. In other words, what makes you stand out from other players)*

My Club team, *(enter name),* will be competing in several large tournaments and I hope you will be able to watch one of my games. Currently, my team is scheduled to play at *(list tournaments).* I will keep you updated about my tournament schedule.

I have attached my soccer resume for your review. I look

forward to staying in touch.

Sincerely,

Your Full Name

Class of (*enter your graduating year*)

City, State

Phone Number and E-mail

Name of Club

Letter Example # 2

Date

Coach's Name

Coach's Full Title

University Name

Address

City, State, Zip

Dear Coach *(Last name):*

I am in my *(enter school year, i.e. Sophomore year, Junior year)* at *(School Name)* High School and will be graduating in June *(year of graduation).* I plan to pursue a degree in *(your major)* and I am very interested in attending *(University's name)* and playing Division *(enter #, i.e. I, II or III)* soccer at your school.

Academically, I have a *(enter number)* GPA and am ranked in the *(enter number)* quarter of my class. I have taken my *(ACT/SAT or both)* and have *scored a (enter #)* on my *(ACT or SAT).*

My position is *(forward, midfielder, defender, etc)* and I play for *(enter Club name).* In addition, *(write about your special qualities such as goals scored, save percentage if GK, awards you have won, highest level you have played at, etc. In other words, what makes you stand out from other players)* Example: I am a Forward, with 2 years State ODP Experience. I average about 2 goals per club *(or high school)* game and have been voted MVP by my teammates.

My Club team *(enter name)* will be competing in several

high-level tournaments and I hope you will be able to watch one of my games. Currently, my team is scheduled to play at (list tournaments). I will keep you updated re: my schedule.

Enclosed is a copy of my HS Transcripts as well as a copy of my *(ACT or SAT)* score. I hope you will have the opportunity to come watch me play. Thank you for your consideration and I look forward to keeping in touch.

Sincerely,

Your Full Name
Class of *(enter graduating year)*
City, State
Phone Number
E-mail

How do I put together a good soccer resume?

A good soccer resume will include:

.....Contact information such as address, phone, e-mail, IM

.....Your high school graduation year

.....Personal information including height, weight, birth date

.....A photograph usually in the top right hand corner, so the coach can identify you on the field. *(preferably a head shot rather than an action shot)*

Academic

.....GPA, class rank, PSAT/SAT/ACT scores.

.....Clubs involved with, awards/honors received, community service performed. *(and for how long)*

Athletics

.....Current club you play for, position you play and jersey number.

.....Previous clubs you've played for *(and dates)*

.....Highest level you've played at. *(i.e. Travel, Premier, State ODP, Regional or National Pool/Team)*

.....Individual high school accomplishments and honors. *(i.e. All Conference, All State, Gatorade Player of the Year, All American, Team MVP, etc)*

.....Soccer details. *(both high school and club)*

.....Team Accomplishments and Schedule

.....At least 2 Coach's Names and their contact information, who will provide your references.

Keep your resume short *(maximum 2 pages)*

Soccer Resume Example

YOUR FULL NAME HERE

Mailing Address   Your Photograph Here
City, State, Zip Code   *(Head Shot only)*
Telephone Number
E-mail Address
Position played: *(i.e. Forward)*
Class of:
(Enter graduating year)

Personal
Date of Birth:
Height: Weight:
Hair Color: Eye Color:

Academic
School Attending:
(Enter name of school)
GPA:
(Enter cumulative GPA to date)
SAT or ACT Scores:
(Enter highest score achieved on either ACT, SAT or both)
Academic Honors:
(Honor Roll and how long, AP classes taken)
Extracurricular:
*(Clubs and how long participated i.e. Class President,
School Newspaper, Debate, etc)*
Community Service:

(Enter any type of Community Service and how long)

<u>Athletic:</u>

<u>Soccer Club:</u>
(Enter Name of current club and how long there. i.e. CFC United U17 2015 - 2019)
<u>Team Accomplishments:</u>
i.e. ECNL, State Cup Champions 2019
<u>Major Tournament Results:</u>
i.e. WAGS 1st place 2019, Disney Showcase 2nd place 2018
<u>Camps:</u>
List noteworthy camps attended.
<u>Coach's Name:</u>
Enter Your Coach's name, phone number and email.
<u>ODP:</u>
List if you have ODP Experience i.e. CT ODP 2016 - 2019
<u>High School:</u>
List your background (i.e. Have started every game on Varsity since freshmen year, list honors received in high school, such as All Conference, Team MVP, All- State, etc)
<u>Other:</u>
List any other sports you play (i.e. Track and Field -Sprinter)
<u>References:</u>
Enter name of other coaches, and their contact information.

** Try to keep your resume to 2 pages or less!

What additional information does a college coach like to see?

Coaches appreciate seeing a copy of your HS transcripts or SAT/ACT scores. If you have any soccer honors *(such as newspaper clippings of you playing particularly well in a game)*, send them along as well.

Is sending a DVD of my soccer highlights worthwhile?

DVDs can get a coach interested in a potential player, but you want one that is well produced. That means no shaky camera, no theme from Rocky, etc. Some coaches only want highlights, other might want to see part of the game. Make certain you identify yourself to the coach *(i.e. I'm #12 on the red team)*.

Some coaches may have time constraints, so identify key moments in the video to make it easier for them to view. Another thing to consider is posting a small video on YouTube and sending the coach the link.

That said, no matter how impressed a college coach may be by an athlete's skill on video, it is unlikely that it will get you recruited on its own. It may catch the coach's interest, but it tells them nothing about the caliber of the team or the opposition. College coaches prefer to watch a player in person, to assess these factors for themselves.

If you want to send a DVD to a college coach, there are two different types: a highlight video and a recruitment video.

The highlight video is generally created to show a player's great plays. It may include shots, tackles, goals, saves, etc., but doesn't necessarily demonstrate the player's real ability and is not an effective recruiting tool.

The recruitment video is longer and has a focus on the game, and the player's contribution to the game. The focus is on content and context, showing the player's range of passing, ability in the air, 1 vs. 1 defending, movement off the ball, speed of play, etc. It is designed to show a coach the player's technical, tactical, and physical attributes without the coach having to be there in person.

If you're an excellent goal scorer, also show your versatility on the field. Demonstrate not only scoring ability, but also your defensive positioning, free kicks, throw-ins, etc. If you're a goalie, since goalies do not normally see a lot of action in games, include footage of you participating in various goalie drills. You could include your goal kicks, punts and throws, as well as your goalie skills on the ground.

You should also include footage of you in goal during a real game. It could be a 20-minute clip or the entire game *(although most college coaches can tell if they like what they see, after 10 - 12 minutes of footage)*. You might want to contact the coach to see what they prefer.

Avoid common mistakes when submitting a DVD, such as zooming out too far *(where the coach can't make out the player and the ball)* or zooming in too close *(where the coach can't see the context of the play, such as focusing in on a player after they've passed the ball)*. Don't send highlights of you just scoring goals, simply dribbling or juggling. The quality of the film should not be low quality or grainy. There is no reason to add cuts, fades and music to the DVD. Make certain that the player is easy to identify in the video.

Send a DVD of a quality game versus a tough opponent: don't send a game that is a blowout.

Make certain that your name, e-mail, club team, jersey number, contact number and graduation year are included.

Is it best to talk to the head coach or an assistant coach?

Most likely, it will be an assistant coach who oversees the initial recruiting. Find out who they are and send them your information. Once they have seen you play and feel that you could potentially be a good fit for their school, the head coach will usually come to see you play.

How will a college coach indicate early interest in me?

They will contact your club coaches to let them know they are interested in you and ask that you call them.

A college coach will come to your games specifically to watch you play, so they can evaluate you in person and learn more about you as an athlete.

Unless you are getting hand-written letters from the coach, chances are that you are not being actively recruited.

Getting information about attending their summer camps does not constitute serious interest.

How will a college coach pre-qualify me for their program?

Besides your athletic ability, coaches will want to make certain that they do not waste their time recruiting you if you do not meet their school's academic standards. They will ask to see your high school transcript as well as your PSAT/ACT/SAT scores, which they will take to admissions for a pre-read if they are seriously interested in you.

What does the information I receive from a college coach mean?

Colleges contact more high school prospects than they make offers to. If a college coach sends information or seems interested, you have to realize they probably have another 25 prospects they are talking to.

Getting letters doesn't necessarily mean you're being recruited. Coaches will send out letters of interest to see which athletes might potentially be interested in their school. However, it is only the first step in a lengthy process.

If you receive general recruiting material from the school, chances are that you are not high on their list.

The more personalized the material, the more interest the coach is showing. Handwritten letters from the coach are a good sign.

Invitations to college summer camps and ID camps do not constitute serious interest, nor does receiving a recruiting questionnaire.

You need to follow up with a college coach to indicate

mutual interest. If you're receiving letters and not responding back to the coach, they will assume you are not interested and move on.

What questions should I ask a college coach on the phone?

A good rule is to practice with schools that are on the bottom of your list, as it will help you become more comfortable talking to your top schools. Show enthusiasm about their program. Act confident, even if you're nervous. Try to lose the 'Ummms.' Make a list of things you want to ask the coach, so you don't forget. Sample questions include:

.....Are you recruiting for *(whatever position you play)* for my spot in *(year you are graduating HS)?*

.....If so, how many players are you considering for that position?

.....What is your recruiting timeline?

.....Is there a good time to come visit your school and meet with you?

NEVER ask a coach about an athletic scholarship without them first indicating interest in having you on their team *(usually that conversation takes place after they've seen you play and are actively recruiting you).*

How much contact should I maintain with a college coach?

Once you establish interest in a particular program with the coach, you should stay in touch with him/her at least once a month, letting them know your tournament schedule and anything else of importance relating to your soccer career. If you're contacting them more than that, most likely you'll be perceived as overbearing, obnoxious or desperate.

What type of information should I keep sending a college coach?

It is important to keep the coach notified of your playing schedule, so that they can come watch you play. In addition, keep them updated with your updated high school transcripts, your ACT/SAT scores and any other athletic honors you receive.

How important is my club coach's recommendation?

If the college coach is contacting your club coach to ask about you, you are on their list of players to potentially evaluate. They will want to find out more about you as an athlete, your character and your work ethic.

Should I fill out a College Recruiting Questionnaire?

If you receive a questionnaire from the college coach, it tells you that you are on the coach's radar, but not necessarily a serious recruit yet. You should fill it out and return it.

Completing a questionnaire also shows the coach that you are really interested in the school. No college contact should be ignored! It's a small world in coaching and you never want to give anyone an opportunity to say something bad about you. If you're not interested in the school, let the coach know, don't ignore him/her.

Upon receiving and reviewing your questionnaire, a college coach will determine if you meet the program's requirements for grades, qualifications, ranking, etc. It's always a good idea in addition to sending the college coaches your resume, to fill out the school's online athletic questionnaire as well.

Should I use a Recruiting service to help me with college coaches?

There are numerous recruiting services. Find out exactly what is offered and check them out if you can. Do they offer services that you can do yourself? Beware of any recruiting service that guarantees you a scholarship. Good recruiting services will explain exactly what they do and what to expect. They will be upfront and tell you that there are no guarantees.

Be cautious of organizations that claim to know the "secrets" of the recruiting process, as there are no special "secrets." If you decide to use a recruiting service, make certain whatever fee you pay gives you value for your money.

Most college coaches do not surf the web looking for talent, so there is no point in using a recruiting service that just posts your profile online. Coaches want to see a letter written by you, not by a service on your behalf.

** *College Coaches want you to take the initiative.*

65

When can a college coach officially contact me?

NCAA rules state that a coach can contact you in writing *(or e-mail)* by Sept. 1st of your Junior year and can only call you by July 1st of your Senior year. Some coaches may send you recruiting material in the form of summer camp brochures or information on their schools during your Sophomore or Freshman year.

What is considered a 'Contact'?

A contact occurs any time a college coach says anything more than hello during a face-to-face contact with a player or his parents off college campus. A contact also occurs if the coach has any contact with the player *(or parents)* at their high school, or any location where they are practicing or competing *(such as a tournament.)* If you see a coach at a tournament, and want to talk to him or her, don't. Again, anything more than a basic hello is considered a contact.

If a college coach talks to a parent or guardian at a showcase tournament, this is considered a contact.

What is the difference between a Contact period and an Evaluation period?

During the evaluation period, a college coach can watch players to evaluate their playing abilities, visit their high schools or where they are playing. They are allowed to write or call student athletes or their parents but cannot have a face-to-face contact off-campus.

During a contact period, a college coach can have a face-to-face contact with a student or their parents as well as visit their high schools and write or call. A coach can watch you compete anywhere as well.

What is a 'Dead' Period'?

A dead period is usually right before the signing period. During a dead period, a college coach may not have any in-person contact with a player or their parents on or off campus. No student-athlete evaluations can be performed either on or off campus as well.

What should I do if a school contacts me and I'm not interested?

If a college coach is interested in you, but it's not a school you can see yourself attending, the polite thing is to be honest and let the coach know. That way they can save time and move on to the next recruit.   It also limits the chances the college coach has negative things to say about you because you've ignored or treated him/her with disrespect. In the close-knit world of college coaching, he/she could be best friends with the coach at your "dream school."

Chapter 6
Visiting a College or University

When should I start my college visits?

It's best to start the college visits as early as Spring of Freshman year, particularly if you're not certain of the type of school you want to attend. Just seeing the campus will give you a "feel" for the school, and whether you can see yourself attending. In addition, if you have many schools you are considering, it's best not to cram in those visits in the span of your Sophomore or Junior years.

When should I contact a coach about my upcoming visit?

Contact the coach with several dates when you could come visit the campus and ask the coach for a meeting. Generally, give them as much notice as possible. Calling a coach a week before is not giving the staff adequate notice.

What is an unofficial visit?

An unofficial visit is a visit to the college at your own expense. They can be taken anytime. Coaches are not allowed to reimburse you for any costs on an unofficial visit (*i.e. food, travel, parking, etc.*) but the Athletic Department can give you 3 tickets to a sporting event. The main benefit in making unofficial visits is it is a great way to learn about the school, the coach and their interest in recruiting you.

How many unofficial visits can I take?

There is no limit on how many unofficial visits you can take at your own expense.

When is the best time to take unofficial visits?

During the fall season, a college coach will be busy coaching his own team. Best time to visit would be in Spring. The coach will have more time to spend with you, to show you their campus and facilities. If they are unavailable, they could have one of his/her players take you on a campus tour.

What happens on an unofficial visit?

An unofficial visit is a chance to see the campus and decide whether you think it would be a good fit for you. If you can, let the coach know in advance you are coming and try to schedule a face-to-face visit. Most times, it will be the assistant coach you first meet with. The only time you cannot talk with a coach during an unofficial visit is during a 'dead period.'

It's best to try and schedule unofficial visits in your Sophomore year. If the school is interested in you as a top prospect, you will find that they spend more time with you. It's not unusual for a potential recruit on an unofficial visit to spend a good part of the day with the Assistant Coach who will give you a tour.

The tour could consist of visiting their athletic facilities, setting up a meeting with an Academic advisor, showing you their fitness facilities, cafeteria, student housing, training facilities, etc.

Bring a photocopy of your high school transcript *(and ACT/SAT scores),* as the coach will also want to see your grades to see if the school is a good academic fit for you. After meeting with the coach, you should have a good feel for their interest level as well as whether you think the particular school could be a good fit for you. If you remain interested, be sure to tell the coaches when they can see you play again.

If an assistant coach doesn't want to spend time with you, and keeps the meeting short, you can assume that you are not high on their potential list of serious recruits.

What is an official visit?

An official visit is any visit to a college by a player that the college pays for. It covers transportation, lodging, and meals for the recruit while they are on their visit. It can be no longer than 48 hours. Many times, the potential player will stay with a member of the soccer team. If a coach wants you to come out for an official visit it usually means you are high on their list of recruits.

When are official visits taken?

Official visits can be taken starting the opening day of your senior year in high school. *(However, make certain you are registered with the NCAA Eligibility Center beforehand.)*

How many official visits can I take?

You may only make one official visit per college and are

allowed a maximum of five official visits to Division I and Division II schools. There is no limit to official visits to Division III and NAIA schools.

What happens on an official visit?

During an official visit, the college can pay for transportation to and from the school for the player, as well as lodging costs plus three meals a day for both the prospect and their parent. Included are reasonable entertainment expenses including three tickets to a home sports event.

Make sure you are on your best behavior on a campus visit, and not just when you are in front of the coaches. Players on a team will be more impressed with a prospect whose behavior is professional and mature.

One of the easiest traps for a player to fall into during an official visit is to get caught up in temptations while socializing during a campus visit, as some recruits want to make a good impression on the older soccer players. However, the impression they need to worry about is on the coach. Word will quickly get back to the coach from the players if your behavior is questionable in any way.

When you're on campus, you'll usually meet other official recruits for your graduating year, get to learn more about the soccer program and get a general feel for the school. It's a realistic way to see what it would be like to be a student-athlete on campus. Finally, always write a thank-you note to the coach and to your host (the person you stayed with), after your visit.

71

When visiting a school, can I practice with the team?

NCAA rules do not permit tryouts with a college team. The college coach can watch you practice, but with your own club or high school only.   NAIA college soccer coaches can invite recruits to train with their team, allowing both the coach and player to see if they are interested in each other.

Chapter 7
What Questions Should I Ask a College Coach on My Visit?

First off, remember that coaches have their own interests in mind when recruiting players, as it is their livelihood. It may be your first time going through the recruiting process, but the coach most likely has gone through it hundreds of times. Make certain you are able to discern the character of the coach. When they recruit you, they may turn on the charm, but look at how they treat their current players.

Ask questions that will help you determine if the school is a good fit. Don't waste the coach's time by asking questions that can be answered on the website. Example:

.....What is the enrollment at *(name of school)?*

.....What majors does your school offer?

.....What is the soccer team's record?

.....What conference is the team in?

You should be able to research this yourself and show the coach you've done your homework about the school and their team.

Bring a pen and paper to take notes. Appearance counts! Make certain you're dressed appropriately. Look the coach in the eye when you give them a firm handshake. If though you may feel nervous, act confident!

Some players start their visits with schools they are less interested in, so they can learn from their mistakes in meeting with a college coach. A potential recruit who asks questions comes across as confident and active in the recruiting process.

To schedule a college visit, send an introduction e-mail, then make a follow-up call to the coach. You could say "Hi Coach *(insert last name)*, I am very interested in *(school name)* and would like to come out on an unofficial visit. Would you be able to schedule some time to meet with me during *(specify which dates)?*

What questions to ask before the coach has seen you play?

.....What style of game do you prefer playing?

    (Coaching style)

.....What do you look for in a *(insert position)* when

    recruiting?

.....How many roster spots do you have available in my year?

.....Of those, how many are in my position?

.....What are your recruiting priorities for that year?

.....How many of your seniors are graduating?

.....How do players compete for playing time in your program?

.....What is a typical day for a student athlete during the

    season and during the off-season?

.....What are the training and conditioning expectations?

.....Is it typical for a Freshman to start?

.....What is your off-season program?

.....What is a typical year for your soccer program?

.....If you're a GK: How much specific training is provided

    to your GK's?

.....Do athletes tend to room together?

.....Is tutoring provided to players if they need help

with homework?

.....Is there mandatory study hall for Freshman year?

.....Do you have Academic advisors?

.....What is the average GPA on the soccer team?

.....What is the graduation rate of your athletes?

.....What is your practice schedule when school starts?

.....What tournaments will you be attending?

.....What is the best way to get evaluated by your staff?

.....What characteristics do you value in your players?

.....What is a typical day of practice like?

.....What are the popular majors on the team?

.....What are your fitness standards for the team during
      pre-season and during the season?

.....Have your players had major injuries over the past
      few years?

.....Am I allowed to make up tests or classes I miss, because
      of the competition schedule?

.....What is the team chemistry like?

What questions to ask after the coach has seen you play at a few tournaments?

.....Where do I stand on your recruiting list or board?
      *(i.e. You're one of 5 forwards he is looking at, but
      number 4 on his/her depth chart)*

.....What would you consider my strengths and weaknesses?

.....Where do you see me on your roster, Freshman year,
      Sophomore year, etc.

.....Would I be red-shirted my Freshman year?

.....When do you expect to make a decision on my position?

.....How do you see me fitting into your program?

.....How many players are you looking at for my spot?

.....Am I under consideration for an athletic scholarship?

.....If so, how long would my scholarship be for?

What questions might a College coach ask me?

.....Why do you want to play for me?

.....What are you looking at majoring in?

.....Have you seen my team play?

.....How much do you know about our team?

.....Do you know what our level of play is like?

.....Do you think you have the skills and ability to play for me? Explain?

.....What kind of impact do you think you'll make on the team?

.....What other schools are you looking at?

.....What schools are currently recruiting you?

.....What position do you prefer playing?

.....Where does our school rank on your list?

.....How are your grades in school?

.....Have you taken your SATs or ACTs?

.....What were your scores?

.....What about our school interests you?

.....What would you consider your strengths to be as a player?

.....How was your club *(or high school)* season?

Be honest with a college coach by letting him/her know what your thoughts are for the future while you visit other schools and speak with other coaches.

Chapter 8

Talking With the Varsity Team Girls on Your Visit

Talk with current Freshmen and Sophomore players to get their perspective on first-year experiences. Is the rest of the team open and friendly, and do they get along well with each other? Watch to see how the girls get along with the coaches. Are there positive interactions? Could you see the team as part of your family for the next four years?

How many hours per day do you practice?

For most Division I programs, expect to practice 2 hours per day, except on game days, plus a few additional 2-hour weight-training sessions per week.

How many days per week do you practice?

Some schools have two practices per day during preseason. Once season and classes begin, practice can be daily, except for game days.

Does the coach discourage you from taking classes in your major, if they conflict with practice?

Although a college coach is technically not allowed to discourage you from taking classes in a difficult major, some coaches will steer away from student athletes if their major requires a lot of additional time spent in lab or research. But then again, would you really want to play for such a coach who puts his or her athletics above your academics?

Do you like the coach?

A coach may seem like a "warm and friendly" when recruiting a player, but you can find out what they're really like by asking existing members of the team. Does he/she treat everyone with respect and fairness? Does he/she genuinely care about his players? Is he/she a screamer on the sidelines? Does he/she allow everyone a chance to fight for playing time or does he/she already have pre-established favorites?

Team players who like and respect the coach will tell you such. They're also the ones who want to win games because they don't want to let their coach down, not just because he/she is going to scream at them.

Do you like the campus and the town you're in?

Is it a safe, friendly, campus? Does the town offer a lot of options for students, such as great *(and affordable)* dining? Is their shopping nearby? Can you get around town easily? etc.

Does the coach use the same 11 players in most games?

If the coach consistently uses the same players, especially in less-challenging games, then it will be difficult to see much playing time. A really short bench isn't a good sign for a positive team environment or long-term improvement.

The best way to see who is getting playing time is to look at the box scores and stats archives of the schools you are interested in, to see how the coach uses their players and subs.

How does the coach determine who plays?

Is it the best players who see time, or does the coach have a core of 'favorite players' that he/she tends to use for most games?

If you don't make fitness standards in preseason, will the coach bench you?

At some schools, if you don't meet fitness standards, the coach will not let you train or practice with the squad until you meet those fitness standards.

You're given enough time to train over the summer to meet those fitness standards, so there is no excuse for coming into preseason camp out of shape. Other schools are a little more lenient, and if players do not pass a fitness test at the beginning of the season, they may be required to do additional training, or to participate in a morning running club.

Chapter 9
What Turns College Coaches Off a Potential Recruit?

Obnoxious parents on the sidelines

Some coaches will make the effort to find out who the obnoxious parents are on the sidelines, to make it a point of "not recruiting" their child. They don't need the headache of these types of parents on the college sideline.

Make sure your parents are not screaming at the team players, being derogatory with the referees, or coaching from the sidelines.

Dealing with Parent Agents

A coach wants to know that the player is seriously interested in their school. Parents who get overly involved in dealing with the coach are seen as a major negative, as the coach is interested in a professional relationship with the player, not their parents.

Nothing turns off a coach more than a parent who wants to take full control of the recruiting process with statements like *"We had a great season. We are applying to Notre Dame, etc."* Don't be a "We" parent. A parent who is too overbearing or controlling might hurt the player's chances of being recruited.

A parent's primarily role is offer support for their child. Do not micro-manage their soccer career. Let your child learn and grow from the experience of dealing with college coaches. A gentle guiding hand is all that is required.

The Diva player

This is the player who thinks they're better than anyone else and shows it with their attitude. They're not a team player and this is demonstrated in their style of play.   They go for individual glory rather than what's best for the team. They blame their teammates, referees, coaches, etc. when things go wrong instead of taking individual responsibility.

College soccer is a team sport, and when a coach sees a 'diva player,' he/she recognizes the potential recruit is not a team player, and in most cases, will take a pass.

Getting form letters or e-mails

There is nothing more annoying than getting an e-mail or letter addressed to "Dear Coach." If you seriously like the college, make the effort to find out the coach's name and personalize your correspondence. Show that you've done your research and know something about the school and the team.

A player not knowing anything about the college

Before you approach a college coach about potentially playing for his/her team, know something about the school. Know your facts.

.....How large is the school?

.....Does it offer the major I am interested in?

.....What are the admission requirements?

.....What is the women's soccer team record?

.....What is the coach's bio?

.....What has been the team's past record and what is

81

their schedule?

This demonstrates to the coach that you've done your research and are serious about attending the school and playing for him/her.

A player with bad grades

Believe it or not, coaches and schools want good students. You should be able to handle the discipline of schoolwork and practice by working hard and keeping up your grades. Be a student first and an athlete second.   If your grades are mediocre when you're trying to get recruited, many coaches will take a pass.

What a student-athlete posts on Facebook or Twitter

You would be amazed at how quickly a negative photo, email or comment can hurt your recruiting chances. Players think "it won't happen to me" or "a coach would never search my Facebook page." However, it can happen to you and a coach doesn't need to have your Facebook access to hear about it.

Each year, there are several college prospects who have had their opportunity to play college soccer greatly damaged by something stupid they've said or posted *(or a picture their friends took and posted).*

It's important to remove questionable photographs. For example, you may be out with friends and not be drinking, but if there is alcohol in the shot, you'll be guilty by association. If you have a photo where you're tired but you look hung over, take it down. Coaches want to see responsible players and having photos of you drunk or even appearing drunk, definitely doesn't send that message.

Make sure you are not writing e-mails, sending messages or leaving posts that are discussing anything inappropriate or being disrespectful. It can happen that a prospect loses their reputation online, because of something someone else wrote. If you have friends who leave inappropriate messages as a joke, ask them to stop.

The soccer community is close. The college coaching community may be competitors, but many of them are also friends. Nearly every single college coach was at one time an assistant with another program, or even a former player. Maintain a good reputation with your club coach, as they will be asked for a reference on your character. Word travels fast. You don't want to find out a school is no longer interested in you, because of an inappropriate posting. Be a positive role model on and off the field.

Chapter 10
Important Things to Consider When Picking a School

Why is College roster size important?

Look at the number of players on the roster. A deep bench indicates that the coach most likely isn't playing everyone and there are many players who are benchwarmers.

Look at the incoming Freshman rosters. If there are a large number of players coming in, are they replacing Seniors who have graduated or is the coach hoarding players? Some coaches have been known to get commitments with promises, or a bit of scholarship money, and then do nothing with the players during their Freshman year. However, those players have been taken off the market for other schools.

Some college rosters show state schools with 35+ players. It's rare for any player ranked 30th on a team, to see much playing time and make any significant impact. Do you want to be part of a large Division I program where you may not see much time and sit on the bench, or would you be happier at a Division II, Division III or NIAC program where you could play and be a more valued member of the team?

What is the turnover rate of players in the school?

About 50% of girls who enter a Division I program will not stay with the program for the full four years. Some will quit soccer and stay at the original school and others will transfer.

The rate is probably higher with Division III schools, as there is no financial incentive for anyone to stay on the team.

Look at how many Juniors and Seniors are on the team. By Senior year, most players that are on the roster are usually impact players, have some type of scholarship or are there because they love being on the team, despite little playing time.

What is the coach's reputation with their team players?

.....Do the players genuinely like and respect the coach?

(A coach who wants respect should also show respect.)

.....Does he motivate his players with his attitude

and enthusiasm for the game?

.....Is he/she a good listener and effective communicator?

...Does he/she treat all players fairly?

.....Is he/she committed to the team and looks out for

the best interest of individual players?

.....Is he/she empathetic and responsive to player differences?

How long has the coach been there?

If a coach has been recently hired, he/she is there to rebuild a team or because the existing coach left for another opportunity. If the coach has been there several years, it is usually because they have a record of success. There are a handful of schools that have long-time coaches, but their team record may be poor: If that's the case, the perception is that those schools are not 100% committed to that particular sport.

Coaching changes occur every year, however, you should look at picking a school for its academics rather than the coach.

How many players does the coach recruit each year?

If a coach brings in 10-12 new Freshmen every year, chances are that he isn't expecting many of those to stick around for the next four years. Knowing where you fit into an incoming group is helpful and you need to know your own personal standing. However, that said, many players and parents are incapable of hearing what they are really being told.

Why should I research the college team?

Looking at the team website is a great way to learn more about the team and the characteristics of players on the roster.

.....What type of background do the players have?

i.e. Is the coach recruiting only players of a certain level, like Regional or National players?

.....Where are the players from?

i.e. Does the coach recruit across the country or primarily in his/her own area?

.....What is the size of the players?

i.e. Does the coach prefer taller players? (particularly important for GK's) or does he have a mix of sizes on the team?)

.....What is their record over the past few years?

.....Which players see the most playing time according to the team statistics?

All this information can help you get a better feel for the team and whether you can see yourself fitting in.

What does it take to play at an Ivy League school?

If you're looking to play at an Ivy League School, your academics should be exceptionally strong. Taking Honors and AP *(Advanced Placement)* classes is a must. Grades should be in the A range, with maybe a few B's. Too many C's can hurt your chances in admissions. SAT/ACT scores must be high. While Ivy League schools *(along with some top universities)* can slightly lower expectations for a top recruit, there are few exemptions for average grades.

If you are focused on the Ivies, you'll need to understand that players have to meet an Academic Index (AI). There is a cutoff point with AI's that they all must adhere to, and no amount of amazing athletic ability will allow you to overcome that. The Academic Index is heavily weighted to standardized testing and is applied to the total of the schools' athletic program. As a result, many schools use their low-end allocations up on big money-making sports *(i.e. football, basketball, etc.)*.

Will I require extra time to complete my degree?

Playing Division I college soccer is time-consuming and it is not unusual for some players to take a lighter load in fall and take summer classes to catch up. Some majors such as pre-med may even need an extra year to finish the program, in order to reduce their academic workload enough to dedicate enough time to play soccer.

If the player has an athletic scholarship, they only have four standard years of NCAA eligibility. If they take longer to finish their studies, they may have to pay the additional college costs themselves.

Chapter 11
Verbal Commitments

What is a Verbal Commitment?

A verbal commitment states publicly one's intention to attend a certain college and is a non-binding, oral agreement between you and the college.

There are two components to this verbal process: the offer and the acceptance. The first part is a college coach's offer to a potential player, for a roster spot, and information as to what the player might expect in terms of an athletic scholarship. In the second part, the player will respond to the college coach with a verbal commitment, confirming interest in attending the college.

When can I make a Verbal Commitment?

A college bound student can announce a verbal commitment at any time. The verbal commitment tells the coach that you intend on joining their program.

If you think this is the college you really want to attend, and this is the best deal you're going to get, then verbally committing early will take the pressure off you for recruitment. Once you make a verbal commitment to a college, the polite thing to do, is to notify the other schools that were interested in you, to let them know you are no longer available.

How binding is a Verbal Commitment?

It is not binding. Only the signing of the National Letter of Intent, accompanied by a financial aid agreement *(athletic scholarship)* is binding on both parties. The verbal agreement is not binding if you have a career ending injury, or there is a coaching change.

What happens if I change my mind after verbally committing?

Even though a verbal commitment is not binding, players who break those agreements are not looked favorably upon. College Coaches make up their future roster based on those verbal agreements.

Can a College coach change his mind after giving me a Verbal Commitment?

Nothing is definite until the National Letter of Intent is signed. However, if a college coach pulls verbal commitments on a whim, word will get out and they will find it difficult to recruit players in the future.

How much time will a College coach give me to verbally commit, if they are interested?

In most situations, when a coach offers a verbal with an athletic scholarship, they will expect a player response in a time period of a few weeks to a few months, depending on the situation. Sometimes, the offer can be for a period of even 24 hours, if the college coach wants to "force" a decision to avoid any extra offers from being received by a player. Be especially aware of offers with no time limit, or "first come, first serve." It is completely possible that the college could recruit other players, while you're deciding and your roster spot is no longer available.

What happens to my verbal commitment if I injured before going to college?

Technically, a coach can pull the scholarship offer if you haven't signed your National Letter of Intent. However, most coaches will not want to damage their recruiting reputation by doing this, so it would be highly unusual for them to cancel the verbal commitment to you, unless you happen to suffer a career-ending injury.

Is there a website that lists up-to-date college commitments?

There is a great website run by a private individual who posts up-to-date verbal commitments which are verified by both player/schools. The website is

https://sites.google.com/site/soccerrecruits.
Updates are posted every few dates and broken down by:

Recent Commitments: *(Every couple of days, new verbal commitments are listed by name of college commitment date, player, position, club, and what school they will be attending)*

High School Graduating Year: *(You can check which players have verbally committed for that particular graduating*

91

year, their playing position, hometown, club and college commitment)

By College: *(Listed alphabetically, you can check which college has recruited which players by name, position, hometown, club, and soccer honors (i.e.. Regional Soccer, National Soccer, ECNL All-Event team, etc)*

By Club: *(Shows which Premier Club's players have committed by name, position, hometown, college commitment, player soccer honors)*

By Event Accolade: *(Shows lists such as NSCAA All-American, Thanksgiving Interregional Rosters (shows which top regional players in the country are selected to compete), Youth National Camp Selections (both US and Canadian), ECNL All-Event Team Selections, World Cup Teams (US and Canada).*

Chapter 12
Athletic Scholarships

Only individual colleges award athletic scholarships, not the NCAA. According to the NCAA, these member schools provide more than $1.5 billion in athletics scholarships annually. Athletic scholarships are also awarded with NAIA and NJCAA Division I. As previously stated in Chapter 1, Athletic Scholarships are as follows:

NCAA Division I

Offers 14 athletic scholarships for women's soccer

NCAA Division II

Offers 9.9 athletic scholarships for women's soccer

NCAA Division III

Does not offer athletic scholarships

(Financial aid or academic scholarships only)

NAIA

Offers up to 12 athletic scholarships for women's soccer

NJCAA Division I

Offers up to 18 athletic scholarships for women's soccer

NJCAA Division III

Does not offer athletic scholarships

Who normally gets an athletic scholarship?

Coaches will give an athletic scholarship to those players who they feel will be impact players and can most likely start as a Freshman.

Most National Team *players (athletes who have*

represented their country at various levels) and Regional players *(players who are in a chosen group from which a National team could be selected for international competition)* will be offered some type of athletic scholarship before others.

Scholarship availability often depends on when the money opens up. If you are interested in an athletic scholarship, check to see who is graduating the year before you will start and if possible, try to figure out how many of those graduating Seniors had scholarships.

It can be important to get just a little money to go to a good Division I program, as this indicates the coach intends to give the player minutes in the first year.

However, remember that lots of top players don't get full rides for many reasons, especially if a coach can get academic or need-based aid to supplement the athletic scholarship.

How do athletic scholarships work?

If on a roster of 25, there are 14 athletic scholarships available, assume that a few players will be non-scholarship and possibly 2-3 per year will be full ride scholarships. The rest of the scholarships will have to be divided amongst the remaining players. Soccer is classified as an "equivalency" sport as opposed to a "head-count" sport. The program is free to divide the 14 full scholarships into smaller scholarship offers.

For example, a team may have 6 players on full scholarships, and 18 more may be on partial scholarships equivalent to 8 full scholarships *(the amounts do not need to be equally divided amongst the remaining 18 players).*

When are athletic scholarships offered?

Athletic scholarships can be offered at any time through a verbal offer. The more coveted players will be offered athletic scholarships earlier, in some cases as early as Sophomore year.

Top colleges will have most of their top offers and athletic acceptances in place, by January of a player's Junior year, and most of the scholarship funds will be committed by Memorial Day in May. By end of high school Junior year, up to 90% of scholarship money will have been allotted by Division I schools.

Most lower level Division I teams, along with Division II teams, will complete their placements during the summer of Junior and Senior year. Division III *(non-scholarship)* programs usually complete their rosters during the summer of Junior year into the first half of Senior Year.

What do athletic scholarships cover?

It will depend on the coach and the school. They can range from full *scholarships (including tuition, fees, room, board and books)* to very small scholarships *(partial tuition, or even something as small as required course-related books).* For the purposes of NCAA compliance, athletic scholarships are only counted against academic fees *(tuition).* It is important to ask the coach if you are getting a percentage-based scholarship, if it includes everything, such as tuition, room and board, books, etc.

Do college coaches usually give full scholarships?

Usually, the only Freshmen who get full rides are those who are outstanding athletes such as National Team players. Most schools give out very few full rides, as it is a large investment in one player, which can potentially cost a team some potential depth on its roster.

What should I expect in terms of an athletic scholarship?

It is common for a coach to divide the scholarships (*i.e. 1/2, 1/3, 1/4, etc*) and increase the scholarship amount as players prove their value to the program. Freshmen generally get the lower scholarships. Full athletic scholarships are rare and usually reserved for the most elite players.

For the most part, players who get recruited early are the ones that usually get the most money. After that, coaches might fill out their roster with additional players, but they generally won't see as much money.

Supposedly, .25 or one-quarter scholarship is a fairly standard award for a new athlete. Upper classmen will typically get more money over time. Many coaches prefer to do this, as a new player is still an unknown commodity and they prefer to reward past performance with established players. Some coaches may offer as little as a few thousand dollars, or even 'books only' scholarships.

Many schools will consider offering a combination of academic aid and an athletic scholarship, as academic money does NOT count against their athletic scholarship total.

Do athletic scholarships change year-to-year?

Athletic scholarships are generally awarded for up to one academic year. The NCAA allows coaches to increase or decrease scholarships each year, but it is unusual for a coach to decrease the player's scholarship if the player continues to fulfill their obligations as a student-athlete. That said, there are some coaches who have canceled a scholarship for poor performance or injury.

Are multi-year athletic scholarships permitted?

According to **BusinessofCollegeSports.com,** new rules were enacted by the NCAA Board of Directors in October 2011, to allow student-athletes multi-year scholarships.

In February 2012, Division I colleges voted on whether to overturn the decision, but it was narrowly defeated.

This now allows schools the option of offering multiyear scholarships *(although the new measure doesn't not require it)*. The majority of Big Ten schools, as well as Auburn and Florida, announced early in 2012, that they will give some incoming athletes' four-year guarantees.

The list of how schools voted is listed below taken from the article *'Which Schools and Conferences Support Multi-Year*

Scholarships', by Alicia Jessop at *BusinessofCollegeSports.com:*

<u>Schools Voting to Allow Multi-Year Scholarships</u>

Arizona State

Atlantic Coast Conference

Auburn

Big East Conference

UCLA

Connecticut

DePaul

Duke

Florida

Georgetown

Georgia

Illinois

Indiana

Iowa

Kentucky

Maryland

Miami

Michigan

Michigan State

Minnesota

Mississippi

Mississippi State

Missouri

Nebraska

North Carolina State

Northwestern

Notre Dame

Ohio State

Oregon

Oregon State

Pac-12

Penn State

Pittsburgh

Purdue

South Carolina

Southeastern Conference

Stanford

UCLA

USF

Utah

Vanderbilt

Villanova

Wake Forest

Washington State

Schools Voting Against Multi-Year Scholarships

Alabama

Arizona

Arkansas

Baylor

Big 12 Conference

Boston College

California-Berkeley

Cincinnati

Clemson

Colorado

Florida State

Georgia Tech

Iowa State

Kansas

Kansas State

LSU

Louisville

Marquette

Oklahoma

Oklahoma State

Providence

Rutgers

USC

St. Johns

Tennessee

Texas A & M

Tech Tech

Texas

Virginia

Virginia Tech

WVU

Wisconsin

Can I lose my athletic scholarship?

Yes, it is possible to lose your athletic scholarship. Things that might lead a player to lose a scholarship would include:

.....If you seriously violate the school's code of conduct
   or engage in inappropriate behavior
   (*i.e. drinking, drugs, etc*) that requires disciplinary action.

.....If you violate NCAA rules regarding amateurism by
   accepting money from boosters or people affiliated
   with the school.

.....If you become ineligible academically by not maintaining
   a certain GPA or by quitting the team.

.....You can also lose your scholarship because of

poor performance on the field. If this happened, you would

be notified in writing and could appeal the decision.

One Division I program for example, cut three freshmen players for violating their rule for underage drinking. The first time, the girls received a warning. The second time they were cut from the team and lost their athletic scholarship. Another school cut 2 players after their first preseason training as the girls came into camp unfit and unprepared: the girls retained their scholarship for the first year but lost it after that.

How is an athletic scholarship renewed?

A college will notify the student-athlete in writing by July 1st, to indicate whether the athletic scholarship will be renewed for the following academic year. Individual schools have appeal policies for athletic scholarships that are reduced or not renewed.

What happens to your athletic scholarship if you are injured in college?

A school will not take back a scholarship because of an injury. You would most likely be red-shirted. However, if the injury ended the career of the athlete, it would be the decision of the coach and the athletic program on how to go forward, after the year ended. However, most good schools will let an athlete who suffers a career-ending injury, keep their scholarship until graduation.

If I'm unhappy at the school and want to transfer, can I go to another school that's willing to offer me money?

NCAA has strict rules regarding this. First off, a player must first get a written "permission-to-contact" release from the school's athletic director before any discussions with a new coach can happen.

You can write to a new NCAA school to let them know you are interested in transferring, but a college coach cannot respond until they receive the written permission-to-contact from your current school. If your current college does not give you a written permission-to-contact, another school cannot contact you to follow up or to encourage you to transfer.

If your request is denied, your current school officials must tell you in writing that you have the right to appeal the decision. If that should happen, a panel of individuals from the current college will conduct a hearing to decide the issue.

If you chose to transfer to a new Division I or Division II school, you cannot get an athletic scholarship for the first year. Discussions are usually formally held during Spring season for the following year.

If you are transferring from a school that is not part of NCAA or NAIA, you do not need written permission-to-contact. At the Division III level, you are allowed to issue your own release and to contact another Division III school about transferring.

Do schools in the Ivy League offer athletic scholarships?

Ivy League *schools (Brown, Columbia, Cornell, Dartmouth, Harvard, UPenn, Princeton and Yale)* even though they are Division I, do not offer athletic scholarships. However, they often have strong financial aid programs for all lower-income and middle-income families, whether the student is an athlete or non-athlete.

If you are looking at playing at the Ivy level, make sure your grades are in order. Without AP or Honors classes, your chances of getting accepted are low. You'll also need a high GPA and great SAT/ACT scores. Although Ivy schools can have slightly lower expectations for a highly recruited player, those exemptions are very small for a select few.

Should my parents get involved in athletic scholarship talks?

A parent should be there to support and guide their child but let the student athlete discuss this directly with the coach. You can be present at this talk, but don't act as your child's negotiator. Let them stand up for themselves when negotiating with a college coach.

Should a player hold out for an athletic scholarship to a school?

Most student athletes would prefer to have an athletic scholarship to a school. However, even without an athletic scholarship, a college coach's support in admissions might mean the difference between getting in, or not.

If the school is one of the player's top choices academically and athletically, then they have to decide whether to attend with whatever athletic scholarship is offered to *(or not)*, or attend a back-up college that might not be in their top choice for a larger athletic scholarship.

Realistically, a player should aim for a school that has good academics and is a great fit, with the athletic scholarship being secondary.

If a coach doesn't bring up an athletic scholarship with you, after having watched you at various tournaments, it's acceptable to ask him/her if you are being considered for a scholarship, or if you should look into any academic scholarships that are offered.

If I'm offered a college scholarship, when should I respond back?

When you get a verbal offer, a college coach will usually give you a deadline to respond back by, which could range from two weeks to a few months. If you are serious about the school and its' program, you should let the coach know sooner rather than later. It's considered poor behavior on the part of the player not to respond at all, as not taking any action may impact other players the coach is considering.

By Senior year, coaches will want an answer quickly, so that if their offer is rejected, they can use that money for other recruits.

Something to be aware of; large offers can substantially decrease when a long time has passed between an offer and an acceptance. If you feel the school is a good fit for you academically and athletically, then you should decide sooner than later. By waiting a few months, you could find the offer is no longer as substantial as before, or worse, is no longer available.

Chapter 13

Your High School Transcript and ACTs/SATs

When should I start to take standardized tests?

A good time to start taking standardized tests is in Spring of your Sophomore year. Besides familiarizing yourself with the pace and format of the ACT or SAT, you will have a base when speaking to a college coach, who will want to see some type of standardized score before they start to seriously recruit you.

What classes do I need to take to play college soccer?

You need to make certain you understand the difference between classes needed to get a high school diploma to get into college, and the core classes that NCAA requires to play college soccer. For example, taking elective classes in things such as art, music, shop, etc. will qualify for your high school diploma, but not towards the NCAA requirements needed to play.

What High School classes are required with NCAA?

For Division I, you will require 16 core classes to meet Eligibility:

.....4 years of English

.....3 years of Math *(Algebra 1 or higher level)*

.....2 years of Natural or Physical Science *(including one year of lab science if offered)*

.....1 extra year of English, math or science.

.....2 years of Social Science

.....4 years of additional core classes *(from the above categories, or in a foreign language, non-doctrinal religion or philosophy).*

Something to be aware of:

check with NCAA to make certain the high school classes you are taking meet their eligibility standards. Remedial classes or classes taught at a slower pace, are not admissible.

As of August 1, 2013, NCAA Division II student-athletes are required to take 16 core classes.

What are the advantages of taking the SAT's?

The SAT generally tests your reasoning and verbal abilities. It was designed as an aptitude test. The SAT has 140 questions plus the required essay. The total testing time is 3 hours and 45 minutes and questions get harder as you progress. You are given 25 minutes to write an SAT essay. Random guessing will hurt your overall score if you have a wrong answer.

Generally, if you do well in English classes, you should do well in the SATs. If you plan on taking an early test *(i.e. Sophomore year),* then the SAT may be a better choice as it tends to be a more intuitive test, whereas the ACT is more curriculum based.

What are the advantages of taking the ACTs?

The ACT measures more what you've learned in school and doesn't have as many theoretical questions. It was designed as an achievement test. The ACT has 215 questions plus an optional essay. The total testing time is 3 hours and 25 minutes. The questions are generally at a constant level of difficulty. The ACT allows less time per question; however, if you answer incorrectly, you are not penalized. You are given 30 minutes to write an essay.

Generally, if you do well in math and science, you should do well in taking the ACT which is all multiple choice.

What are the biggest differences between the SAT and ACT?

The ACT has a science section with questions in biology, chemistry, earth science and physics. The science section is looking for your ability to read and understand graphs, scientific hypotheses and research summaries. The ACT will have a few questions that require trigonometry, while the SAT does not. You should understand how to use sine and cosine.

Regarding writing an essay for either the ACT or SAT, a SAT essay prompts tend to present a broad issue that you need to write about, using examples from history, literature or personal experience. An ACT essay asks you to take a stand on a controversial issue and explore the counterargument as part of your essay.

SAT Critical Reading places more emphasis on vocabulary than the ACT English sections. Some students find that if they have good language skills, but average vocabulary, the

ACT is easier.

What do you need to know when taking the SAT or ACT?

Students taking either test should know that grammar is important. You should know the rules for proper pronoun usage, subject/verb agreement, identifying run-ons, etc. The ACT places more emphasis on punctuation and includes questions on rhetoric strategies.

PSAT scores correlate closely to SAT scores. On average, SAT scores are generally 150 points higher on the current PSAT scale.

What are the average scores for SATs and ACTs?

Each section of the SAT is out of 800 points *(for a total of 2400),* whereas the ACT sections are out of 36 points. Scores are weighted, so it's difficult to get a perfect score on either exam. Average score for the ACT is generally around 21 *(36 is the highest score),* and about 500 on each section for the SAT.

Official SAT or ACT test scores are no longer accepted from high school transcripts and must be sent directly from the testing agency to NCAA.

Should I take Honors and/or Advanced Placement classes?

Absolutely. You don't need to take all Advanced Placement and Honors classes, but you should be able to show that you can handle higher-level classes and aren't afraid to challenge yourself in doing so.

How important are my grades for admission if I'm playing college soccer?

Many athletes believe that soccer alone can get them into a good school. Athletic ability can give you a major boost, but grades still count.

Admissions want to see an athlete who can maintain good grades while competing on the soccer field. If you're a poor student in high school, chances are you'll be a poor student in college. Admissions want to know that a player is making an effort in their studies. You don't need perfect A's, but you should be taking classes that challenge you, such as Honors or A.P.

Some admissions officers work directly with athletic recruitment and will pre-qualify a player based on their grades and SAT/ACT scores. A coach may have 3-4 top forwards they are considering with different GPAs and SAT/ACT scores, and the admissions officer will tell him which players are likely to get in. Pre-qualifying is defined as "making certain their academics" meets the school's minimum requirements to get in.

Taking it a step further, a coach can support some players more heavily in admissions than others. This is called the preferential pool. The lower down you are in the pool, the better your academics must be.

What do I need to play at an Ivy League School?

You should be taking Honors and Advanced Placement classes in high school, with consistent high grades throughout. Test scores *(SAT/ACT)* should be considerably above average.

The Ivy League does not offer athletic or merit scholarships, only need-based financial aid. Athletes and potential recruits must meet the "Academic Index" requirements. This is a calculation based on GPA and SAT scores. This limits the number of "low scorers" that can be accepted, which means that some athletes cannot be recruited, no matter how talented they are.

If the college has a potential recruit with low scores and GPA, it will usually recruit an athlete with higher scores and GPA to "balance" the class *(although that particular player may not see much playing time.)*

Overall, most players who do get recruited have high grades and high scores *(and coaches will prequalify a candidate before actively recruiting them).*

111

Chapter 14
A Parent's Role

Should my parents contact college coaches on my behalf?

Absolutely not. The coach is recruiting the player, not the parents. If a college coach continually receives numerous phone calls from a parent, a coach will start to believe they are a nuisance and may not bother recruiting their child. A parent agent is considered a red flag, which could mean an unenthusiastic or unmotivated recruit.

College coaches want to hear from the player and are impressed by students who initiate a conversation. You need to make the effort to contact the coach yourself, as it tells them that you're interested and enthusiastic about their program.

Can my parent's behavior hurt my college recruiting chances?

An obnoxious parent can hurt your chances of being recruited. Coaches want talented players, but they also want good, ethical parents. They don't need a player whose parents are always second- guessing or constantly calling them. You're competing against a wide pool of players, and if your parents are being difficult, the coach will move on.

Make certain your parents are also not obstinate in scholarship negotiations. It should not be the first thing you bring up in a meeting with a college coach. Parents can cause a recruit to be dropped from a list if a coach feels the parent is too difficult (i.e. constantly calling or e-mailing the coach, continually complaining, acting obnoxious or challenging the coach).

No matter how talented the athlete is, no college coach wants to deal with an out-of-control parent.

What do my parents need to know?

Create an environment that fosters positive growth and stop putting pressure on your child. Try not to be a helicopter parent! If your child is an exceptional athlete, keep them humble. If a player receives too much attention, they can develop attitude problems. They are the ones who think they will sail by because they are top student-athletes, only to learn a hard lesson later in life. Make certain your child maintains a high academic standard. Classroom performance will tell a college coach a lot about the player's work ethic and dedication.

A player's character is very important. Make sure your child makes good decisions off the field as well. You can tell a lot about the player's character by the company they keep. Make sure they are accountable for their actions.

A coach wants to see a player who they know can contribute to the team, and not bring a negative attitude or inappropriate behavior.

Chapter 15
Admissions Support

How much support should I expect from a college coach regarding admissions?

Generally, a coach will pre-qualify a student athlete with admissions before actively recruiting the player. If the player is a top recruit, the coach may use some of their influence with admissions, but it is usually only reserved for a few (2-3) players. Coaches may have a longer list of players they are recruiting, but usually only use their top support for certain athletes.

A player with grades and test scores far below normal standards, may find it difficult to get into a top academic school, even with the coach's support.

What is an Ivy Likely Letter?

A Likely Letter is a letter from admissions after a thorough review of the player's completed application. It means that admissions are committing to admit that applicant to the school, barring the standard caveats for all admissions *(being expelled, poor grades, etc.)*.

A college coach has to want a player badly enough to request the Likely Letter from Admissions. It's a golden ticket. For a player, the Likely Letter can come as early as October *(in Senior Year)*, relieving the stress of not knowing if they will get in Early Decision. If a coach is unwilling to give you a Likely Letter, you're generally not considered one of his top recruits.

114

If you are an extraordinary player academically, the coach may try to save a Likely Letter for someone more on the bubble academically. However, that puts you at a disadvantage and you should insist on the Likely Letter. By receiving one, you are also agreeing in advance to attend the University and withdraw all other college applications.

A great book that explains strategy issues in detail at the Ivy's is "**Reading the Game: Inside Athletic Recruiting in the Ivy League**" by Chris Lincoln, who played football at Dartmouth.

What is a 'College Tip'?

A college tip is also known as coach's support, pick, etc. These are general terms that mean the coach goes to admissions and requests a slot to get a weaker *(academically)* player in. A coach might have 4 tips *(slots) but* be able to only get 2 Likely Letters from admissions.

What is the difference between Early Decision and Early Action?

Early Decision allows students to apply early a school, and if you are accepted, it is usually a binding decision. *(Check the policy at each individual school).* It shows the school that you really want to attend, and usually helps improve your chances of being accepted in admissions.

Early Action allows students to apply early to schools, but the decision is not binding.

Chapter 16
The National Letter of Intent (NLI)

What is a National Letter of Intent?

The National Letter of Intent is an agreement that spells out what you are going to receive to play soccer for that particular school. Depending on the agreement, it can be vague (i.e. 1/3 of costs) or numerically specific *(i.e. You will receive $52,550 for the year to cover tuition, fees, room and board, and books).*

Once you sign a National Letter of Intent, all other schools are obligated to cease recruiting you. Furthermore, signing a National Letter of Intent does not guarantee you playing time. You also agree to attend that college for one year.

<u>If you are under the age of 21, then your Letter of Intent also must be signed by your parent or guardian.</u>

In addition, according to NCAA, letters can't be signed by a recruit before 7 a.m. *(local time where the recruit is located)* on the first day of the signing period. If a letter is submitted without a time of signature, the Letter of Intent is considered invalid. Coaches cannot talk about recruits before having a valid National Letter of Intent on file. This avoids the "one-upmanship" that could occur between coaches in the recruiting process.

Recruits have 14 days to sign a National Letter of Intent from the date it is issued to them. This period allows players time to think about their decision. Institutions have 21 days from receipt of a signed National Letter of Intent to file it with the conference office.

How is the National Letter of Intent sent to me?

Only the college recruiting you will send you the National Letter of Intent. It can be sent to you by regular mail, courier, email or fax. *The material you receive must include an offer of your athletic scholarship for the entire academic year.*

Is my College Coach be present when I sign my National Letter of Intent?

No. NCAA rules state that any in-person, off-campus contact made with a prospect for the purpose of signing a National Letter of Intent, or attendance at the signing, is prohibited. A coach is also not allowed to personally deliver the National Letter of Intent to you off-campus. However, there is nothing that prevents you from receiving a National Letter of Intent while on campus, although you may only sign during the permissible signing period.

Is an athletic scholarship the same thing as a National Letter of Intent?

No, but many players confuse them with each other. By signing a National Letter of Intent, a future NCAA player ends the recruiting process with all other institutions and commits to the college for a year. In return, the student-athlete is guaranteed a one-year scholarship from that school (the athletic scholarship is sent as a separate Financial Agreement from the school to the athlete, usually included with the NLI).

When do I sign a National Letter of Intent?

A National Letter of Intent is signed usually in spring of Senior year by every player who receives an athletic scholarship. Generally, the signing day starts the first Wednesday in February.

If I complete my college playing season, have I fulfilled my National Letter of Intent?

You must complete the entire academic year at the college in order to fulfill the National Letter of Intent obligation.

What happens if I change my mind after signing a National Letter of Intent?

According to NCAA, to get a release after signing a National Letter of Intent, a prospect must fill out paperwork and give a specific reason for not wanting to follow through on their commitment.

Some schools will grant releases without question and others have a policy that requires the recruit to appeal to the committee of commissions. The committee generally requires some sort of extenuating circumstances before granting a release.

It is possible for another school to recruit you only if you have received a complete release or had the National Letter of Intent recruiting ban lifted by the school where you signed. The lifting of the ban must be indicated on the NLI Release Request Form.

NCAA rules state that a student-athlete who signs with a school but does not fulfill an academic year *(defined as two semesters or three quarters),* will lose one year of competition in all sports and must serve one year in residence at their next school.

So, in a nutshell, if you break your NLI, you do not have to attend the school, but you cannot play for another program the following year or accept a scholarship during that time.

What happens if my coach leaves for another program after I sign my NLI?

The National Letter of Intent still remains binding if the coach leaves after you've signed, as you are signing with a college, not a specific coach.

Chapter 17
NCAA

What is the NCAA?

NCAA stands for the National Collegiate Athletic Association. It was founded in 1906 and overlooks athletics as the governing body for over 1,300 colleges, universities, conferences and organizations.

The NCAA is made up of three classifications which are Division I, II and III, each with its own rules regarding personnel, recruiting, eligibility, amateurism, benefits, financial aid and playing/practice seasons. It is based roughly on school size and each division has conferences for regional league play.

Only Division I and Division II schools can offer athletic scholarships. NCAA dictates the maximum number of scholarships that a school can dispense in any one sport.

Many Division III schools are private liberal arts colleges and routinely award financial aid and potential merit money for students who have athletic talent.

What are the NCAA rules regarding recruiting?

In order for a player to be part of a college team, they must qualify through the NCAA. you must
1) be considered an amateur and
2) you must qualify academically.
College bound players may participate in amateur sports as long as they do not receive expenses in excess of travel,

lodging or equipment for practice or competition. NCAA doesn't give you any leniency for not knowing the rules.

What is the NCAA Eligibility Center?

Formerly known as the NCAA Clearinghouse, the Eligibility Center makes certain that as an amateur athlete, you have not been paid to play or indirectly received monetary benefits in return for your play *(beyond reasonable expenses)*, or played with paid players in a league considered professional by the NCAA.

Regarding academic qualifications, your indexed high school GPA and SAT/ACT scores must meet NCAA standards. It is a sliding scale, so the higher your GPA, the lower your SAT/ACT scores can be. You also need to submit transcripts that show you have taken enough of the correct courses *(see below)*.

When should I register with the NCAA Eligibility Center?

Athletes should register online with the NCAA Eligibility Center the beginning of the junior year in high school at www.eligibiltycenter.org.

How do I register at the NCAA Eligibility Center?

Click the link to enter as a NCAA College-Bound Student Athlete. You then need to click the "New Account" button at the top right of the screen.

You will need to provide a valid e-mail address to create the account and start the registration process.Make certain the e-mail address stays with you even after you complete high school. In the next section, you will need to give your name, address, date of birth and gender.

In the section titled "My Coursework," you will need to enter the name and location of the high school you currently attend in this section. If you have attended more than one high school, you will need to have that information ready as well.

In the section titled "My Sport", you will select the sport you plan to participate in at the DI or DII college level. The NCAA Eligibility Center will ask you about the high school and/or club teams you have been a part of, and events you have participated in during your high school career.

You will be asked to answer several questions about your sports participation history, to give the NCAA a better idea of your amateur status and to identify any potential issues that might conflict with NCAA rules such as

1) salary for participating in athletics,

2) prize money,

3) contracts with a professional team,

4) tryouts, practice or competition with a professional sports team,

5) benefits from an agent or prospective agent,

6) Agent representation,

7) Delayed initial full-time college enrollment to participate in an organized sports competition.

If you are a Division I Qualifier, you will be able to receive an athletic scholarship during your first year of college, practice and compete for your college during your first year and play four seasons in your sport if you continue to maintain your eligibility year to year.

If for some reason, you become a Division I Non-Qualifier with NCAA, you will not be able to receive an athletic scholarship your first year (although you can still receive need based financial aid) and you won't be able to practice or compete with the college the first year of school.

Payment

Your account will be complete once you send in a registration fee of $65 (or $95 for International students). You must pay online by credit card, debit or e-check.

Double check that the courses you have taken so far match your school's list of NCAA courses.

What happens after I register with the NCAA Eligibility Center?

Take the ACT, SAT or both. When sending the scores to the NCAA Eligibility Center, use code "9999" as the score recipient.

Ask your high school guidance counselor to send an official transcript to the NCAA Eligibility Center after completing your Junior year. If you have attended more than one high school, the NCAA will require official transcripts from all high schools attended.

The NCAA Eligibility Center does not accept faxed transcripts or test scores.

During your Senior year, request final amateurism certification on or after April 1st (for fall enrollment) or October 1st (for Spring enrollment). After graduation, ask your high school guidance counselor to send your final transcript to the NCAA Eligibility Center with proof of graduation.

What happens if I need to talk to the NCAA?

They can be reached at

NCAA

P.O. Box 6222

Indianapolis, IN 46206-6222

(317) 917-6222

Hours: 12:00 – 4:00 p.m. EST, Monday through Friday

NCAA Eligibility Center

Certification Processing

PO Box 7136

Indianapolis, IN 46207-7136

(877) 262-1492   (for US Callers, toll free)

(317) 223-0700   (for International Callers)

(317) 968-5100 (Fax)

Your eligibility is your responsibility *(Ignorance is no excuse!)*

Do NCAA requirements apply if I want to play Division III soccer?

Division III players are not certified by the NCAA Eligibility Center as there are no initial-eligibility requirements in this division and each school sets their own admission standards.

Division III has shorter playing and practice seasons, no red-shirting or out-of-season games and has a focus on regional in-season and conference play.

Chapter 18
Different Types of Schools and Programs

What does it take to play Division I soccer?

Division I soccer is the most prominent of all levels, where the majority of athletes aspire to play. Many of the players that play Division I soccer play for high-level club teams and play at high level tournaments. Many have ODP experience, such as State Team, Regional Team/Pool or National Team/Pool. Their high school experience could include All Region/Conference/Sectional, All-State, All-American, or being a Varsity Starter.

Playing Division I soccer requires more of a time commitment, with more mandatory training time. The competitiveness is usually on a higher level.

Many Division I players start to get recruited in their Sophomore or early part of their Junior year. Playing in Division I requires athletes to be cleared by the NCAA Eligibility Center.

How many athletic scholarships are offered in Division I women's soccer?

Division I women's soccer programs have a maximum of 14 FTE (Full-time Equivalent) athletic scholarships available.

Which Colleges offer Division I women's soccer?

(See Chapter 25)

What does it take to play Division II soccer?

The Division II schools are typically smaller than Division I, but there are some great Division II teams that could easily beat some Division I teams in competition. Typical players on a Division II roster have club experience and have been high school varsity starters. Some will have ODP experience as well. Division II recruits must be cleared by the NCAA Eligibility Center.

How many athletic scholarships are offered in DII women's soccer?

DII Women's programs have 9.9 FTE (Full-time Equivalent) athletic scholarships available.

What does it take to play Division III soccer and do they offer athletic scholarships?

There are some Division III schools who would be competitive with some lower level Division I schools.   Division III coaches rely largely on players to make the initial contact with the school to let them know that they are interested in their program. There are about 100+ Division III program in New England and New York. Your academic record is more important than your athletic talent. These schools can't give you an athletic scholarship, but they can give you a merit scholarship, financial aid, or help you with other programs *(i.e. get you a job as a resident advisor, which comes with free room and board).* There are some outstanding small liberal arts colleges, as well as large universities in Division III.

No Division III programs make a big effort to compete with Division I schools for recruits. In Division III schools, the player will be playing for the love of soccer as athletic funding is not available. The typical Division III player will usually have club experience and most likely will have been a high school varsity starter.

The academics are the main focus and you experience more of a "normal" college experience. Travel to play games is generally more local. Depending on the league your college is in, you'll probably travel by bus about half the weekends.

Division III schools make very few offers prior to senior year, although they can express keen interest. Because there is no athletic scholarship and no National Letter of Intent, the recruiting process can seem much slower. The time commitment for a Division III program is a couple hours of practice each day, with a game on weekends.

What is NAIA?

NAIA stands for the National Association of Intercollegiate Athletics. Most of the NAIA schools are smaller, private schools who are competitive in both athletics and academics.

They have nearly 300 members colleges and universities in the U.S. which offer college sports for nearly 60,000 athletes where approx. $450 million in financial aid *(tuition, room and board, books)* is awarded between 13 sports.

If you play for a NAIA school and feel that the team or school is not the right fit for you, you can transfer to another

NAIA school without having to sit out the following year. The NAIA competition level is probably comparable to an average NCAA Division II school.

To be eligible to participate in NAIA, besides graduating from High School two of the following three requirements must be met:

1. Have a 2.0 (C) or higher cumulative GPA average in high school
2. Achieve a minimum of 18 on the ACT or 860 on the SAT
3. Graduate in the top-half of your high school class.

There are fewer restrictions regarding contact. NAIA college soccer coaches can invite recruits to train with their team, allowing both the coach and player to see if they are interested in each other. Students are permitted a maximum of two days of tryouts on a campus visit throughout their entire career, and the tryout cannot interfere with school time.

In the NAIA, a student-athlete must be enrolled at least 12 hours every semester. If a player is not happy at one institution, she can transfer to another without being penalized athletically. You must register with the NAIA Eligibility Center and have your high school send transcripts, as well as contact the ACT or SAT to send test scores directly (the NAIA code is 9876).

Registration costs for U.S. students is $65 and for International students, it is $95. The NAIA is different from the NCAA, each having their own sets of rules and certification processes. Student-athletes who have completed their junior year in high school and have at least a 3.0 GPA *(along with an 18 ACT or 860 SAT score)* may obtain an eligibility determination before graduating from high school. Contact information is:

NAIA Eligibility Center
P.O. Box 15340
Kansas City, MO 64106
Phone: (816) 595-8300
Toll Free: (816) 881-6242
Email: ecinfo@naia.org
Website: http://www.naia.org

Does NAIA women's soccer offer Athletic Scholarships?

NAIA Women's programs have 12 athletic scholarships available. As with NCAA, scholarships can be full or split *(i.e. half an award, 1/4 award, etc.)* Currently, the NAIA does not recognize letters of intent, however, some NAIA conferences do.

What is NJCAA?

NJCAA stands for the National Junior College Athletic Association. Besides lower tuition costs, two-year Junior or Community colleges offer an opportunity for players not ready yet for 4-year schools or academics.

NJCAA schools in DI offer full or partial scholarships, while Division III schools are not allowed to.

The advantage of playing a sport in NJCAA is that their admissions standards are not as strict. You will be able to play soccer for 2 years while working towards your college degree.

Contact information for NJCAA is:

NJCAA National Office

1631 Mesa Ave.

Suite B

Colorado Springs, CO 80906

Phone: (719) 590-9788

Fax: (719) 590-7324

Website: http://www.njcaa.org

How many athletic scholarships are offered in NJCAA women's soccer?

NJCAA Women's Soccer programs *(Division I)* have 18 athletic scholarships available. Eligibility requirements vary school to school, and you should contact the athletic dept. at the school you are interested in attending.

General requirements are that a prospective student-athlete must be a high school graduate either through receiving a high school diploma or having passed their GED *(General Education Development Test)*. Players are allowed to have two seasons of competition and must be attending full-time while playing.

What is NCCAA?

NCCAA stands for the National Christian College Athletic Association and consists of Division I and Division II schools.

Many NCCAA colleges are also NCAA or NAIA members, but only NCCAA DI schools offer athletic scholarships.

What is NESCAC?

NESCAC is the only conference *(Division III)* that does not allow its athletes to play their sport out of season. Many NESCAC schools also bar students from playing more than one sport.   The priority is a good education, not to be a full-time athlete, therefore, athletic scholarships are not offered.

NESCAC schools are Amherst, Bates, Bowdoin, Colby, Connecticut College, Hamilton College, Middlebury, Trinity, Tufts, Wesleyan and Williams. All offer excellent academics. Most NESCAC schools don't travel long distances to see potential recruits, except for some tournaments.   PDA Memorial Day weekend tournament is the one that seems to attract a large amount of NESCAC coaches.

What is required to play college soccer if I am an International Student?

Since coaches usually don't have a travel budget for international recruiting, make certain you contact college coaches to let them know of your interest in playing for them at their school. A DVD of your soccer highlights can act as an introduction and generate interest as well. Have a full-game video available as well to send, if the coach requests it. If possible, attend college summer camps or guest at a tournament recruiting showcase if you can afford to.

You will be required to take the TOEFL *(Test of English as a Foreign Language)* Exam if you are a non-native English speaker. It is best to download the NCAA International Standards Guide to check your country listing, to make certain that you are studying to get a certificate that meet's the NCAA's core course requirements.

At NAIA schools, potential foreign player-athletes *(graduates of high schools outside the United States)* must provide their academic records in their native tongue, as well as a certified, word-for-word English translation.

Chapter 19
High School vs. Club Soccer

Do college coaches recruit from watching high school games?

Very few Division I coaches will place a lot of importance on high school play. They want to see a player compete at the highest level possible, and at high school, the competition is inconsistent and difficult to assess. Players are different ages and have different soccer backgrounds. Coaches prefer to see a player at a showcase tournament, competing against other similar-caliber teams the same age.

In addition, most high school play takes place in fall, which is the time that college coaches are busy with their own teams. Coaches at local or smaller colleges (such as Division III) will consider high school players, but playing high school soccer only, will make it more difficult for you to be recruited at larger Division I schools.

Do college coaches have a preference re: club soccer vs. high school soccer?

Playing for a club will help give you a huge advantage in the recruiting process. Many college coaches believe that if a player is truly committed to playing college soccer, they will play at the highest level they can. They consider club soccer to be the way to evaluate players as the level of play is generally more competitive.

Club soccer also allows a coach to focus in on a particular recruiting class, so that when they go to a showcase

133

tournament, they are able to see players that will be graduating high school at the same time, for the most part. Club soccer also competes year-round, making it easier for a coach to attend events, as there is no conflict of game schedules.

Good soccer clubs will have a record of developing players to compete at the college level. They will attend important showcase tournaments that allow their players to be seen by many college coaches. Good club coaches will help you in your recruiting effort by making phone calls on your behalf. That said, don't expect a club coach to exaggerate your playing ability with a college coach, as the club's *(and his/her)* reputation is on the line.

Can my club coach or high school coach help me with recruitment?

College coaches will call your club coach or high school coach for a reference on you, if they are seriously interested in recruiting you as a player. College coaches place a lot of weight on your club coach's opinion. Who better to give them an honest evaluation than your club coach who has seen you play in dozens of games and practice sessions?

Don't expect your club coach to give you an amazing recommendation if you don't deserve it as his/her reputation is on the line with the college coach. If your club coach is not truthful, it hurts their credibility with future recruits for the college.

Most college coaches will prefer talking to your club coach directly about your skills, attitude and work-ethic rather than reading a letter of recommendation. Remember to keep your current coach updated on your progress with college recruiting.

Chapter 20
Summer College Camps and Winter ID Camps

Are college summer camps worth the investment?

Many college coaches put together summer camps to generate revenue. Most likely, there will be hundreds of players attending. You will need to be one of the best players at the camp to have a chance to be recruited at most higher-level Division I schools.

The advantage of attending summer camps is that colleges coaches will usually get to see you play over a 4-7 day span in multiple games.

It's not unusual for some college Division I camps to have Division III college coaches assisting as well, for cross recruitment. The players that the Division I coach may take a pass on could be the ones that the Division III coach would love to have play on their team. Larger camps are usually separated into several teams, depending on the player's level.

Are college soccer ID clinics worthwhile attending?

College ID camps are a great way to play in front of a college coach without the major expenses of a summer camp.

Many college coaches like the fact they are able to see multiple players competing against each at one location and time who are seriously interested in their school. It offers the coach an opportunity to see a player's technical and individual skills. If you are truly an elite athlete and able to show it, you should be able to get the college coach's attention.

However, just because you've been invited does not mean you're a serious prospect. Some schools use these as moneymakers. Is it an open clinic or is there a set limit on the number of prospects attending?

If you really want to find out if the coach is serious about recruiting you, ask if you can attend as a prospect without paying the fee, and see what the reaction is.

For Division III schools, going to a college soccer ID camp may be the best way to be seen and evaluated for potential recruitment by the college coach.

Do college coaches really recruit players from camps?

There are success stories where players have impressed the college coach to the point where they have been recruited to play on a Division I team.

However, most recruitment takes place at showcase or tournament events, where coaches are watching players compete in the same age bracket, against similar talented teams.

The one exception to the rule seems to be NESCAC (and some Division III schools), as their camps are used for screening and recruiting players.

How can I figure out if a camp is worthwhile attending?

For Division I schools, has the coach displayed serious

interest in you beforehand? Have you had previous contact with the school and made unofficial visits? Has the coach come to see you play at showcase tournaments? Is the camp an open clinic or is it by invitation only? How many players will be attending? If you attend a camp or a clinic, you want to make certain that you will get seen by the college coach. It is difficult to specifically showcase your skills if there are hundreds of players attending with different levels of ability.

Chapter 21
College Recruiting Showcase Tournaments

How important are college recruiting showcases?

College recruiting showcases are a major way of getting a college coach interested in you. It's of major importance to get them to see you play, so that they might evaluate and consider you for their program. You must get yourself on a college coach's radar at the schools you are interested in, or they will not know you exist.

Even if you attend multiple college showcase tournaments each year, if you have not contacted college coaches to let them know that you are interested, they won't know who you are and won't come to see you play.

Occasionally, they will 'discover' a player at a tournament, by it doesn't happen often.

Since the level of competition is strong at these tournaments, by attending a college showcase, a coach gets to see you in your natural environment with your teammates. They get to evaluate your size, athleticism, style of play, speed, technical skills and your impact on the team.

Most top showcases are usually invitational. The idea is to allow all players on a team to play, and to gain exposure to college coaches. Usually there are no playoffs or finals and games are usually once per day.

Find out which coaches will be attending, such as the head coach or assistant coach. Remember that according to NCAA rules, college coaches are not allowed to speak directly to players *(or their parents)* at these showcase tournaments.

What are some of the top recruiting showcases?

Some of the top recruiting showcases include:

...ECNL/USSF League Events

...PDA Memorial Day Showcase *(New Jersey)*

...Surf Cup *(California)*

...Disney Showcase *(Florida)*

...Score at the Shore *(North Carolina)*

...Jefferson Cup *(Virginia)*

...WAGS *(Maryland)*

...MSSL/MAPS events *(New Jersey)*

...Dallas Cup *(Texas)*

...Las Vegas College Showcase *(Nevada)*

When should I contact a college coach regarding a showcase tournament?

College coaches can watch hundreds of prospects during a showcase tournament weekend. This involves a lot of planning, so it's best to let them know that your club team will be playing at this showcase well in advance *(i.e. 2-3 weeks before)*.

What should I send a college coach regarding my attendance at a showcase?

Send the coach an email with the days you will be playing, what team you will be playing against, the time you will be playing, and on what field. In other words, make it as easy as possible for them to come see you play. Your e-mail can state something like:

Hi Coach Smith:
     My team will be playing in a few weeks at the College Invitational and I'm excited about being there. If you are planning on attending this tournament, I hope you will take the time to see me play. My team's schedule is as follows:

Saturday, June 1st   9:00 a.m. vs. Eagles Premier, Field 1 at *(list location)*
Sunday, June 2nd   10:00 a.m. vs.Hawks Premier, Field 2 at *(list location)*

     I'm very interested in *(insert name of college)* and I hope that after you see me play, you'll find that I could be a good fit for your team. Thanks so much for your time.

Taylor Johnson
Jersey #
(Name of premier soccer team)

     If any of the times or fields change after you have emailed the coach, send them an immediate update.

What should I expect at a college recruiting showcase?

     If a coach is seriously considering you for their program, expect to see them at the sidelines watching part of your games. It's important to find out if the college coach will be there in order to give your club coach a heads-up that they will be watching, and to make certain you are playing on the field. A college coach will usually watch only 1/2 of the game before moving on to watch another player.

What will a college coach be looking for, when they watch you at a showcase?

The coach will get to see your play in your environment with your teammates. They will get a sense of your style of play and they can evaluate your impact on a team.

To be successful at a tournament, you must learn to ignore the college coaches that are on the sidelines. Try to relax and focus on playing. Don't start trying to impress them and most importantly, if you make a mistake, don't dwell on it. College coaches know everyone makes them. It also shows the coach how the player responds to adversity.

Remember that you are always on display. Whether on the field, during warm-ups or even walking in the parking lot, be professional. Don't give a college coach a negative impression by doing something "childish" to turn them off.

Should my club team have a recruiting brochure to give to college coaches at showcase?

Most premier teams have recruiting brochures *(player profiles)* to hand out to a college coach who comes to watch the team play. These will usually include all the contact information of the players participating, as well as the club coach's contact information in case a college coach wants to request further information on a player.

The team cover page should include:

.....Upcoming Tournament Schedule

.....Team Achievements

.....Coach's contact information

The player profiles should include:

.....Player name and uniform number

.....Position played

.....Photo of player *(Head shot... not an action shot)*

.....Height, Weight, Birthdate

.....Home phone, cell phone and e-mail address

   (listing your home address is optional)

....High School GPA, SAT or ACT results

If you have the room, include additional information such as:

.....Athletics: High School Sports, Club Sports, Awards or

   Recognitions

.....Academic Information: Awards, Achievements, Honors

.....Coach Reference(s)

The back of the player profile book could include:

...A team picture with roster of team with player numbers.

Team parents should be positioned at every corner of the field to hand out brochures to coaches, as well as keep record of who attended. At the end of the showcase tournament, a list should be generated to the player and his parents of which college coaches were watching their game. This allows the player to follow up with the coach.

Should I send a thank-you note to the college coaches who have come to see me play?

Absolutely. A college coach will have many players they are looking at during a college showcase. If they've taken the time to come see you play, you should send them a thank-you note. By sending a note it reconfirms to them, your interest in attending the particular school.

Some players take the time to send a thank-you letter rather than a thank-you note. This differs in that the letter will also ask the coach what they thought of your performance and whether the coach could see you fitting into their program. The letter could mention a potential visit to the college in the future, asking if the coach could meet with you.

If your team is attending another showcase in the future, the player should invite the coach to that as well. It is important to maintain an ongoing dialogue with a coach, without being too pushy.

After a coach has seen you play a few times, you should be able to determine if there is sincere interest on their part in pursuing you. Sometimes it's better to receive a 'not interested' from the coach, then a series of 'maybes' from coaches who may be just keeping their options open.

Is it a good idea to guest at College Recruiting Showcases?

If your team is not playing the major club tournaments or college showcases, find a team that is looking for a guest player so that you can attend the event. You should double-check with the club coach to find out what position they intend to play you before you agree to be a guest player. There is nothing worse than being a Forward, then being asked to play an entirely different position that you're not comfortable with, in front of a college coach.

If you can practice with the team a few times before guesting, it will make it more comfortable for you and the teammates as you will get to know them and their playing style.

Chapter 22

Life as a College Soccer Player

What are the perks of being a college athlete?

Going into college as a freshman can be daunting, but as an athlete, you will have immediate "built-in" friendships with fellow team members. It will provide you with a structured environment which helps make the transition from high school to college easier.

Student athletes often receive extra benefits from their school such as exclusive use of athletic facilities, and academic advisors who work exclusively with athletics. Some schools offer early registration for athletes and the ability to move into housing early.

When does college preseason begin?

It depends on each individual college, but generally most Division I schools start their preseason the first week in August. Ivy League schools start a little later, generally mid-August.

Do Freshmen see a lot of playing time?

It depends on the school and how deep their roster is. In the larger Division I schools, incoming Freshmen do not play a lot unless they are incredible players or there is a spot that needs to be filled through graduation or injury.

Can I walk-on to a college soccer team?

To be a walk-on is harder than getting recruited. You need to be accepted academically by the college and then try out for the team. Depending on the caliber of the program, coaches may allow a player to try out for the team and then make a decision. Be aware that it is a difficult thing to accomplish, although not impossible. You would pretty much have to be an impact player for the coach to consider you, or on the other side of the coin, a practice player. It's harder to make the soccer team as generally, by the time the Fall Session of school starts, a college coach will already have his/her roster due to recruitment and may not need extra players.

Walk-ons do not typically get athletic scholarships. They can expect normal stipends during training, uniforms, travel expenses covered when with the team, etc. They do not sign Letters of Intent and walk- on commitments are not publicized on NLI signing day.

What should I expect with the speed of play in college?

Playing in college is like nothing before. It's fast-paced, demanding and a lot more physical than club or high school play. Expect daily practices and fitness training which could be year-round if you play Division I. You will have curfews before game days and are expected to keep up your studies, even with a demanding athletic schedule.

Just because you've been a star on your High School or Club team, it doesn't mean you will immediately be so on your college varsity team. Most likely, your teammates will all have been star athletes as well.

What will a typical year be like as a college athlete?

If you are playing Division I, it is important to remember that usually there is no "Off Season." You will be working out with the team and on your own, year-round.

During fall, expect daily practice usually early in the morning or late afternoon for about 1 ½ - 2 hours per day. In addition, expect to work with a strength and conditioning coach usually 2 -3x/week for about an hour each time. Fridays and Sundays are usually game days and Saturday (depending on the school) is usually a light 1-hour workout. Mondays are usually days off. Individual training sessions are not unusual to meet specific needs of players.

Once fall season is over, the team enters a conditioning stage where players work out with the strength and conditioning staff 4-5 days per week. Players can expect to continue individual training sessions with the coaches to improve specific areas of their game.

During the spring season, many college teams resume daily team practice with games against local university teams scheduled on weekends. Usually the spring season finishes 1 week prior to final exams.

What is a Student- Athletic Code of Conduct?

Each school has their own Student-Athlete Code of Conduct that the player is expected to sign. It sets out the expectations of student athletes, such as their behavior and academic responsibility.

It is important to note that student-athletes are held to a higher standard of personal conduct as they represent their school and are subject to greater public scrutiny. Good sportsmanship and a respectful manner are expected of all players.

A Student-Athletic Code of Conduct will stress that you act in a manner that will not embarrass you or the college. College sanctions may be imposed for misbehavior. Student-athletes can be suspended or dismissed from participating in sports for any of the following:

.....Unlawful possession or consumption of alcohol.

.....Possession of any illegal drug.

.....Unauthorized steroid use.

.....Academic dishonesty.

.....Arrest for any crime

   (minor traffic offenses are usually not included)

.....Fighting, threatening, or harassing any individual.

If you are a recruited athlete, your scholarship could be cancelled or not renewed for any act of misconduct that may occur.   Some schools may even require player athletes to pay back all tuition and fees covered by the athletic scholarship. In some cases, students can be dismissed from the team or even the school, depending on the severity of the transgression.

What are the fitness standards in college?

Fitness standards vary college to college, but make no

mistake about it, coaches expect you to come into preseason fit and healthy. You will generally be given a summer preseason workout *(usually late Spring)* to help you prepare, so there is no excuse for not meeting fitness standards. Running a one or two mile is standard, and you may be expected to do it within a certain time, along with a beep test and shuttle runs.

A lot of new freshman procrastinate on their training for college until the last minute, and then expect to meet the fitness goals in just 2-3 weeks of training. As a result, they come into preseason camp out of shape, or come in with an injury from overexertion. If the coach expects you to work out for 8 weeks prior to camp, following a specific schedule, do it!

If you don't meet your preseason fitness standards, you've already hurt yourself with the coach. Some coaches, if you don't meet their fitness expectations, will bench you. Other players, who repeatedly fail the team's fitness tests, can be cut from the team.

What should I expect in college play?

If you've been a star player on your club or high school team, chances are the players on a college varsity team are at or above your level. Expect to fight for playing time, even if you were a starter before. There are no guarantees and your coach will expect you to make an immediate impact when you join the team.

Players need to make an impression in their freshman year. If they don't, it gets tougher each year afterwards. If they're not playing a lot of minutes, they could be considered on the bubble and the coaches could already be looking at a future replacement.

There is also pressure surrounding starting spots. You will be competing against older players and incoming younger players. If you don't see a lot of minutes as a Freshman (unless your red-shirted), it will probably not change much when you are an upperclassman.

Even if you see major playing time, there is no guarantee it will continue. From a personal point of view, my daughter was a freshman player who started all college games, set single season GK records at Univ. of Michigan, was ranked 8th in the nation for Save % and GAA and took her team to the NCAA Elite 8 tournament. She was benched her sophomore year in favor of a new incoming freshman. NOTHING IS GUARANTEED! (When that happened, she applied to transfer to Univ. of Louisville where she successfully played her last 2 years)

How many players usually dress and travel with the team?

There are limits on travel rosters. If a game involves plane flights and hotel rooms, not all players will go. For budgetary reasons, many schools will impose travel roster restrictions (generally set at 18).

Making the "travel team" is one of the more stressful situations that new players will face, who have not yet established themselves. If a game involves single day bus trips, the entire roster can travel. However, many conferences limit the number of players allowed to dress for a game, so even if a player "travels", they may not dress.

Some coaches will let the players know by posting a travel list, while others meet with them individually to tell them the 'good' or 'bad' news. When you travel with the team, generally the Athletic Dept. will provide the college professors with a list of players and the approved travel dates that the players will be absent. Be aware, that they can be some tough professors that don't honor the excused absence and will hold it against players.

What does it mean to be red-shirted?

To be red-shirted means that the athlete is taking the year off from playing competitively, but is still officially on the team, is allowed to practice with them and is attending classes.

Sometimes incoming Freshmen who would not see much playing time during their first year, are red-shirted *(which must be declared at the beginning of the season),* as are injured athletes *(who would miss a major portion of their season).* Athletes who are red-shirted have an extra year *(or two)* to complete their studies.

If I don't like my college, can I transfer to another school to play?

First off, do not talk to another school's college coach, until you know about the rules about receiving written permission. Do not tell the coach you are quitting the team, rather that you are asking for a "permission to contact" only.

For the most part, NCAA transfer rules allow a one-time transfer, although if you transfer within a conference, you may have to sit out one year. That said, it is completely up to the college whether to grant a complete release. Generally, it is easiest when you transfer out of your conference.

If your current school does not give you the necessary written "permission-to-contact," another school cannot contact you or encourage you to transfer. You are still able to transfer to another school; however, if the new school is Division I or Division II, you will not be able to receive an athletic scholarship until after your first year there.

Should you decide to transfer from a Division III program to a Division II or I program, there is no requirement that states a player has to be at the school for any given period, before scholarship money is made available on the transfer. Again, it's best to review NCAA Transfer Guidelines for up-to-date information.

The typical scenario for a college player to transfer, will involve approaching their coach and the athletic dept. about a release usually in spring semester. The college can provide two types of releases.

The general release basically allows the player to contact – or be contacted by any program and reopens the recruiting process.   The second release limits the players to certain specific schools.

If a school denies your release, you can petition the NLI Policy and Review Committee for such a release. In order to do so, you need to provide of copy of the NLI Release Request Form, signed by the Director of Athletics, stating "No

Release/" Once this paperwork is submitted, the Committee will consider your request. Obtaining a release in spring, may also impact an athlete as the coach may decide to exclude the player from spring training, games and athletic facilities.

For further clarification, contact the NCAA Eligibility at www.eligiblitycenter.org or call them at (877) 262-1492.

If I signed a National Letter of Intent and then get a complete release, can I sign another NLI in the same year?

No. National Letter of Intent policy states that a player is only permitted to sign one valid NLI in an academic year. If you sign an NLI during an early period and get a complete release before spring signing period ends, you are not permitted to sign a second NLI in the spring. You must wait until the net academic year to sign another National Letter of Intent.

What happens if I don't like my college coach?

Sometimes this happens as players realize that their coach is nothing like they were during recruiting. A coach may turn on the charm to their "high scholarship players" to impress them, but they can be a Jekyll/Hyde personality otherwise.

At this point, you have to make the decision to get along with them for the year. If you still can't stand them after that point and dread being part of the team because of the coach, it might be time to consider transferring to a different program.

Can an athletic scholarship be withdrawn or reduced?

A coach cannot withdraw athletic money during the academic year after the contract is signed, unless there is a serious violation of the Student Athlete Code of Conduct.

How will a college coach decide an athletic scholarship the following year?

Usually, at the end of the fall season, the head coach will sit down and have meeting with each player to discuss and review their season's performance. Sometimes, the coach can include a written evaluation as well. It gives both parties an opportunity to discuss the spring season schedule and expectations. It is during this session that the player's athletic money can be discussed for the following year.

If the coach has not scheduled any one-on-one meetings, the player should ask to sit down with the coach to discuss the topic. If a player sees their scholarship reduced, it is usually because the coach is unhappy with the player's performance relative to the team's performance and doesn't feel the amount of money being spent on that particular player is warranted.

What happens if my college coach leaves?

When a college coach leaves, players will find they have to prove themselves all over again to the new head coach. Expect to be evaluated, as new coaches have new playing styles and requirements. Most players will never see a major change in their athletic money, but those who do need to be financially *(and emotionally)* prepared.

How does a college coach decide who to play?

Coaches are impressed by players who come into pre-season fit and in shape. These athletes work hard and are dedicated. They are as intense in practice as they are in games. They're team players and play as such. In most situations, these athletes who will perform well in training, are fit and focused, will most likely make the starting squad and be impact players.

What academic support is available to student athletes?

Each school will vary in the academic support they provide, but many colleges provide student athletes with support services such as class scheduling and advising, tutoring when needed, computer labs and special monitored study halls. Freshmen players are generally monitored by an Academic Counselor who checks their class attendance and stays on top of their grades. Usually study hall is mandatory the first year. If a student-athlete is maintaining a high GPA, then may switch out of study hall.

Chapter 23
RPI Rankings and APRs

What is an RPI ranking?

According to the NCAA, a RPI ranking stands for Rating Percentage Index. It is a measure of strength of the playing schedule and how a team does against that schedule. It is one of the many factors that NCAA sports committees use when evaluating Division I teams for postseason selection, seeding and bracketing. Division II and Division III schools do not use RPI data.

According to NCAA, a team's RPI consists of three factors that are weighted:

1. Division I winning percentage, 25% of the RPI
2. The opponent strength of the schedule, 50% of the RPI
3. The opponents' opponent strength of the schedule, 25% of the RPI

NCAA's RPI starts the season with every team exactly equal, unlike some other formulas that create "preseason" ratings for each team. Therefore, an RPI cannot be compiled until teams have played at least one contest.

A more detailed explanation can be found at:
http://www.ncaa.org/wps/wcm/connect/public/NCAA /Championships/NCAA+Rating+Percentage+Index/

What is an APR (Academic Progress Rate)?

An APR *(also known as the Academic Performance Rating)* is a standard determined by the NCAA to measure the success or failure of college teams at moving student-athletes toward graduation.

The APR is calculated by allocating points for eligibility and retention, the best indicators of graduation. It is designed to measure academic progress semester-by-semester throughout the school year. It is a composite team measurement based on how individual members do academically.

Teams that don't make the 925 APR requirement *(which is equivalent to a 50% graduation rate)* are subject to sanctions and penalties which range from scholarship reductions to severe sanctions such as restrictions on scholarships and practice time. A perfect score is 1,000.

To look up a particular school and how their athletes perform, the link is:

http://web1.ncaa.org/maps/aprRelease.jsp

One thing to be aware of is that the APR only applies to students receiving athletic scholarships, not all varsity athletes at a university.

Chapter 24
The NCAA Tournament

Currently, NCAA Women's Soccer Championships are divided into three divisions. The tournament field for Division I currently consists of 64 teams. Colleges who win their conference get an automatic berth in the championships. The remaining 32 teams have at-large bids.

The at-large teams are selected by a committee which uses a number of criteria, the most influential being the RPI *(Ratings Percentage Index),* which objectively compares the results and strength of schedule of all Division I teams.

First round is generally grouped by geographical proximity. Winners of the last eight years of the NCAA Women's Soccer Championship tournaments include:

2019
National Champion:
Stanford *(defeated North Carolina in 2 OT, PKs)*

2018
National Champion
Florida State *(defeated North Carolina 1-0)*

2017
National Champion
Stanford *(defeated UCLA 3-2)*

2016

National Champion

Southern California *(defeated West Virginia 3-1)*

2015

National Champion

Penn State *(defeated Duke 1-0)*

2014

National Champion:

Florida State *(defeated Virginia 2-1)*

2013

National Champion:

UCLA *(defeated Florida State 1-0)*

2012

National Champion:

North Carolina *(defeated Penn State 4-1)*

2011

National Champion:

Stanford *(defeated Duke 1-0)*

2010

National Champion:

Notre Dame *(defeated Stanford 1-0)*

Chapter 25

Division I Colleges for Women's Soccer

* Division I offers Athletic Scholarships

Women's College Conferences

America East

American Athletic (AAC)

Atlantic 10

Atlantic Coast (ACC)

Atlantic Sun

Big 12

Big East

Big Sky

Big South

Big Ten

Big West

Colonial Athletic Association

Conference USA

Horizon League

Independent

Ivy League

Metro Atlantic Athletic Conference

Mid-American

Missouri Valley

Mountain West

Northeast

Ohio Valley

Pacific 12

Patriot League

SEC

Southern

Southland

Southwestern Athletic

Summit League

Sunbelt

West Coast

Western Athletic

Chapter 26 - Great Soccer Web Sites

www. NCAA.org

National Collegiate Athletic Association offers extensive information recruiting, rules compliances, Division I, Division II, Division III and academic requirements for athletes.

http://www.playnaia.org/page/eligibility.php

Information about playing in NAIA.

http://www.njcaa.org

Information about playing in Junior College.

www.Collegeboard.com

Information to help you with your college search with information on individual schools and their admission requirements.

https://sites.google.com/site/soccerrecruits

Up-to-date information on verbal commitments to colleges for women's soccer as well as which colleges have recruited players for which year.

http://talk.collegeconfidential.com

Information about the college search, admissions, college essays, financial aid & scholarships, college life.

http://search.espn.go.com/high-school-soccer

Information on girls' high school soccer, recruiting and college commitments.

http://Topdrawersoccer.com

Information about college soccer, HS recruits, clubs, standout individual players, ECNL.

http://www.bigsoccer.com/community/forums/womens-college.66

Information about women's college soccer including individual schools, recruiting and coaching changes.

http://www.informedathlete.com

Rick Allen, a former NCAA Compliance Director with over 25 years' experience provides advice on many issues, including transfers, waivers/appeals, eligibility issues, scholarship strategies, etc.

(On a personal note, when my daughter wanted to transfer from Michigan, Rick provided invaluable in providing advice)

National Collegiate Athletic Association (NCAA)

700 W Washington Ave

PO Box 6222

Indianapolis, IN 46206-6222

P: 317-917-6222

www.ncaa.org

NCAA Eligibility Center (Clearing House)

PO Box 7136

Indianapolis, IN 46207

Phone: (877) 262-1492

International Callers: (317) 223-0700

Fax: (317) 968-5100

www.ncaaclearinghouse.net

National Association of Intercollegiate Athletics (NAIA)

1200 Grand Blvd

Kansas City, MO 64106

Phone: 816-595-8300

Fax: 816-595-8301

Toll Free: (866) 881-6242

www.playnaia.org

National Junior College Athletic Association (NJCAA)

NJCAA National Office

1755 Telstar Drive, Suite 103

Colorado Springs, CO 80920

P: 719-590-9788

F: 719-590-7324

www.njcaa.org

National Christian College Athletic Association (NCCAA)

302 W Washington St

Greenville, SC 29601

P: 864-250-1199

F: 864-250-1141

www.thenccaa.org

Author Biography

Lucia Bucklin was involved with the world of soccer recruiting for the over six years with her two daughters. By writing this book, she hopes other athletes and their parents can benefit from her experiences and her mistakes regarding the world of college soccer recruiting.

Her oldest daughter was recruited to play women's soccer at Brown University while her youngest daughter was recruited to play soccer at University of Michigan before transferring to Univ. of Louisville.

She currently lives in South Florida with her 7 dogs and is actively involved in writing, photography and animal rescue.

Made in the USA
Columbia, SC
25 October 2021

47777334R00095